interchange

FIFTH EDITION

T0372629

2A

Student's Book

Jack C. Richards

with Jonathan Hull and Susan Proctor

WITH DIGITAL PACK

CAMBRIDGE
UNIVERSITY PRESS

Shaftesbury Road, Cambridge CB2 8EA, United Kingdom

One Liberty Plaza, 20th Floor, New York, NY 10006, USA

477 Williamstown Road, Port Melbourne, VIC 3207, Australia

314–321, 3rd Floor, Plot 3, Splendor Forum, Jasola District Centre, New Delhi – 110025, India

103 Penang Road, #05-06/07, Visioncrest Commercial, Singapore 238467

Cambridge University Press & Assessment is a department of the University of Cambridge.

We share the University's mission to contribute to society through the pursuit of education, learning and research at the highest international levels of excellence.

www.cambridge.org
Information on this title: www.cambridge.org/9781009040709

© Cambridge University Press & Assessment 2013, 2017

First published 2013
Fifth edition 2017
Fifth edition update published 2021

20 19 18 17 16 15 14 13 12 11 10 9 8 7

Printed in Great Britain by CPI Group (UK) Ltd, Croydon CR0 4YY

A catalogue record for this publication is available from the British Library

ISBN 978-1-009-04049-5 Student's Book 2 with eBook
ISBN 978-1-009-04050-1 Student's Book 2A with eBook
ISBN 978-1-009-04051-8 Student's Book 2B with eBook
ISBN 978-1-009-04069-3 Student's Book 2 with Digital Pack
ISBN 978-1-009-04070-9 Student's Book 2A with Digital Pack
ISBN 978-1-009-04071-6 Student's Book 2B with Digital Pack
ISBN 978-1-316-62269-8 Workbook 2
ISBN 978-1-316-62270-4 Workbook 2A
ISBN 978-1-316-62271-1 Workbook 2B
ISBN 978-1-108-40709-0 Teacher's Edition 2
ISBN 978-1-316-62228-5 Class Audio 2
ISBN 978-1-009-04072-3 Full Contact 2 with Digital Pack
ISBN 978-1-009-04073-0 Full Contact 2A with Digital Pack
ISBN 978-1-009-04074-7 Full Contact 2B with Digital Pack
ISBN 978-1-108-40306-1 Presentation Plus 2

Additional resources for this publication at cambridgeone.org

Informed by teachers

Teachers from all over the world helped develop *Interchange Fifth Edition*. They looked at everything – from the color of the designs to the topics in the conversations – in order to make sure that this course will work in the classroom. We heard from 1,500 teachers in:

- Surveys
- Focus Groups
- In-Depth Reviews

We appreciate the help and input from everyone. In particular, we'd like to give the following people our special thanks:

Jader Franceschi, **Actúa Idiomas,** Bento Gonçalves, Rio Grande do Sul, Brazil

Juliana Dos Santos Voltan Costa, **Actus Idiomas,** São Paulo, Brazil

Ella Osorio, **Angelo State University,** San Angelo, TX, US

Mary Hunter, **Angelo State University,** San Angelo, TX, US

Mario César González, **Angloamericano de Monterrey, SC,** Monterrey, Mexico

Samantha Shipman, **Auburn High School,** Auburn, AL, US

Linda, **Bernick Language School,** Radford, VA, US

Dave Lowrance, **Bethesda University of California,** Yorba Linda, CA, US

Tajbakhsh Hosseini, **Bezmialem Vakif University,** Istanbul, Turkey

Dilek Gercek, **Bil English,** Izmir, Turkey

Erkan Kolat, **Biruni University, ELT,** Istanbul, Turkey

Nika Gutkowska, **Bluedata International,** New York, NY, US

Daniel Alcocer Gómez, **Cecati 92,** Guadalupe, Nuevo León, Mexico

Samantha Webb, **Central Middle School,** Milton-Freewater, OR, US

Verónica Salgado, **Centro Anglo Americano,** Cuernavaca, Mexico

Ana Rivadeneira Martínez and Georgia P. de Machuca, **Centro de Educación Continua – Universidad Politécnica del Ecuador,** Quito, Ecuador

Anderson Francisco Guimerães Maia, **Centro Cultural Brasil Estados Unidos,** Belém, Brazil

Rosana Mariano, **Centro Paula Souza,** São Paulo, Brazil

Carlos de la Paz Arroyo, Teresa Noemí Parra Alarcón, Gilberto Bastida Gaytan, Manuel Esquivel Román, and Rosa Cepeda Tapia, **Centro Universitario Angloamericano,** Cuernavaca, Morelos, Mexico

Antonio Almeida, **CETEC,** Morelos, Mexico

Cinthia Ferreira, **Cinthia Ferreira Languages Services,** Toronto, ON, Canada

Phil Thomas and Sérgio Sanchez, **CLS Canadian Language School,** São Paulo, Brazil

Celia Concannon, **Cochise College,** Nogales, AZ, US

Maria do Carmo Rocha and CAOP English team, **Colégio Arquidiocesano Ouro Preto – Unidade Cônego Paulo Dilascio,** Ouro Preto, Brazil

Kim Rodriguez, **College of Charleston North,** Charleston, SC, US

Jesús Leza Alvarado, **Coparmex English Institute,** Monterrey, Mexico

John Partain, **Cortazar,** Guanajuato, Mexico

Alexander Palencia Navas, **Cursos de Lenguas, Universidad del Atlántico,** Barranquilla, Colombia

Kenneth Johan Gerardo Steenhuisen Cera, Melfi Osvaldo Guzman Triana, and Carlos Alberto Algarín Jiminez, **Cursos de Lenguas Extranjeras Universidad del Atlantico,** Barranquilla, Colombia

Jane P Kerford, **East Los Angeles College,** Pasadena, CA, US

Daniela, **East Village,** Campinas, São Paulo, Brazil

Rosalva Camacho Orduño, **Easy English for Groups S.A. de C.V.,** Monterrey, Nuevo León, Mexico

Adonis Gimenez Fusetti, **Easy Way Idiomas,** Ibiúna, Brazil

Eileen Thompson, **Edison Community College,** Piqua, OH, US

Ahminne Handeri O.L Froede, **Englishouse escola de idiomas,** Teófilo Otoni, Brazil

Ana Luz Delgado-Izazola, **Escuela Nacional Preparatoria 5, UNAM,** Mexico City, Mexico

Nancy Alarcón Mendoza, **Facultad de Estudios Superiores Zaragoza, UNAM,** Mexico City, Mexico

Marcilio N. Barros, **Fast English USA,** Campinas, São Paulo, Brazil

Greta Douthat, **FCI Ashland,** Ashland, KY, US

Carlos Lizárraga González, **Grupo Educativo Anglo Americano, S.C.,** Mexico City, Mexico

Hugo Fernando Alcántar Valle, **Instituto Politécnico Nacional, Escuela Superior de Comercio y Administración-Unidad Santotomás, Celex Esca Santo Tomás,** Mexico City, Mexico

Sueli Nascimento, **Instituto Superior de Educação do Rio de Janeiro,** Rio de Janeiro, Brazil

Elsa F Monteverde, **International Academic Services,** Miami, FL, US

Laura Anand, **Irvine Adult School,** Irvine, CA, US

Prof. Marli T. Fernandes (principal) and Prof. Dr. Jefferson J. Fernandes (pedagogue), **Jefferson Idiomass,** São Paulo, Brazil

Herman Bartelen, **Kanda Gaigo Gakuin,** Tokyo, Japan

Cassia Silva, **Key Languages,** Key Biscayne, FL, US

Sister Mary Hope, **Kyoto Notre Dame Joshi Gakuin,** Kyoto, Japan

Nate Freedman, **LAL Language Centres,** Boston, MA, US

Richard Janzen, **Langley Secondary School,** Abbotsford, BC, Canada

Christina Abel Gabardo, **Language House,** Campo Largo, Brazil

Ivonne Castro, **Learn English International,** Cali, Colombia

Julio Cesar Maciel Rodrigues, **Liberty Centro de Línguas,** São Paulo, Brazil

Ann Gibson, **Maynard High School,** Maynard, MA, US

Martin Darling, **Meiji Gakuin Daigaku,** Tokyo, Japan

Dax Thomas, **Meiji Gakuin Daigaku,** Yokohama, Kanagawa, Japan

Derya Budak, **Mevlana University,** Konya, Turkey

B Sullivan, **Miami Valley Career Technical Center International Program,** Dayton, OH, US

Julio Velazquez, **Milo Language Center,** Weston, FL, US

Daiane Siqueira da Silva, Luiz Carlos Buontempo, Marlete Avelina de Oliveira Cunha, Marcos Paulo Segatti, Morgana Eveline de Oliveira, Nadia Lia Gino Alo, and Paul Hyde Budgen, **New Interchange-Escola de Idiomas,** São Paulo, Brazil

Patrícia França Furtado da Costa, Juiz de Fora, Brazil Patricia Servín

Chris Pollard, **North West Regional College SK,** North Battleford, SK, Canada

Olga Amy, **Notre Dame High School,** Red Deer, Canada

Amy Garrett, **Ouachita Baptist University,** Arkadelphia, AR, US

Mervin Curry, **Palm Beach State College,** Boca Raton, FL, US

Julie Barros, **Quality English Studio,** Guarulhos, São Paulo, Brazil

Teodoro González Saldaña and Jesús Monserrrta Mata Franco, **Race Idiomas,** Mexico City, Mexico

Autumn Westphal and Noga La`or, **Rennert International,** New York, NY, US

Antonio Gallo and Javy Palau, **Rigby Idiomas,** Monterrey, Mexico Tatiane Gabriela Sperb do Nascimento, **Right Way,** Igrejinha, Brazil

Mustafa Akgül, **Selahaddin Eyyubi Universitesi,** Diyarbakır, Turkey

James Drury M. Fonseca, **Senac Idiomas Fortaleza,** Fortaleza, Ceara, Brazil

Manoel Fialho S Neto, **Senac – PE,** Recife, Brazil

Jane Imber, **Small World,** Lawrence, KS, US

Tony Torres, **South Texas College,** McAllen, TX, US

Janet Rose, **Tennessee Foreign Language Institute,** College Grove, TN, US

Todd Enslen, **Tohoku University,** Sendai, Miyagi, Japan

Daniel Murray, **Torrance Adult School,** Torrance, CA, US

Juan Manuel Pulido Mendoza, **Universidad del Atlántico,** Barranquilla, Colombia

Juan Carlos Vargas Millán, **Universidad Libre Seccional Cali,** Cali (Valle del Cauca), Colombia

Carmen Cecilia Llanos Ospina, **Universidad Libre Seccional Cali,** Cali, Colombia

Jorge Noriega Zenteno, **Universidad Politécnica del Valle de México,** Estado de México, Mexico

Aimee Natasha Holguin S., **Universidad Politécnica del Valle de México UPVM,** Tultitlàn Estado de México, Mexico

Christian Selene Bernal Barraza, **UPVM Universidad Politécnica del Valle de México,** Ecatepec, Mexico

Lizeth Ramos Acosta, **Universidad Santiago de Cali,** Cali, Colombia

Silvana Dushku, **University of Illinois Champaign,** IL, US

Deirdre McMurtry, **University of Nebraska – Omaha,** Omaha, NE, US

Jason E Mower, **University of Utah,** Salt Lake City, UT, US

Paul Chugg, **Vanguard Taylor Language Institute,** Edmonton, Alberta, Canada

Henry Mulak, **Varsity Tutors,** Los Angeles, CA, US

Shirlei Strucker Calgaro and Hugo Guilherme Karrer, **VIP Centro de Idiomas,** Panambi, Rio Grande do Sul, Brazil

Eleanor Kelly, **Waseda Daigaku Extension Centre,** Tokyo, Japan

Sherry Ashworth, **Wichita State University,** Wichita, KS, US

Laine Bourdene, **William Carey University,** Hattiesburg, MS, US

Serap Aydın, Istanbul, Turkey

Liliana Covino, Guarulhos, Brazil

Yannuarys Jiménez, Barranquilla, Colombia

Juliana Morais Pazzini, Toronto, ON, Canada

Marlon Sanches, Montreal, Canada

Additional content contributed by Kenna Bourke, Inara Couto, Nic Harris, Greg Manin, Ashleigh Martinez, Laura McKenzie, Paul McIntyre, Clara Prado, Lynne Robertson, Mari Vargo, Theo Walker, and Maria Lucia Zaorob.

Plan of Book 2A

1 Good memories

▸ **Ask questions to get to know people**
▸ **Discuss childhoods**

1 SNAPSHOT

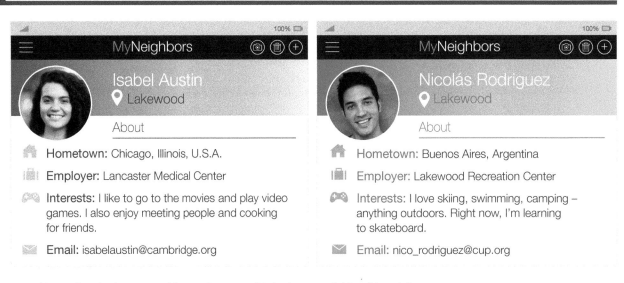

Nicolás and Isabel are neighbors. Do you think they could be friends?
What social media sites do you belong to? Which one is your favorite?
Create your own online profile and share it with your classmates. What things do you have in common?

2 CONVERSATION Where did you learn to skateboard?

▶ **A** Listen and practice.

Isabel: Oh, I'm really sorry. Are you OK?
Nico: I'm fine. But I'm not very good at this.
Isabel: Neither am I . . . . Hey, I like your shirt. Are you from Argentina?
Nico: Yes, I am, originally. I was born there.
Isabel: Did you grow up there?
Nico: Yes, I did, but my family moved here 10 years ago, when I was in middle school.
Isabel: And where did you learn to skateboard?
Nico: Here in the park. I only started about a month ago.
Isabel: Well, it's my *first* time. Can you give me some lessons?
Nico: Sure. Just follow me.
Isabel: By the way, my name is Isabel.
Nico: And I'm Nico. Nice to meet you.

▶ **B** Listen to the rest of the conversation. What are two more things you learn about Isabel?

3 GRAMMAR FOCUS

▶ **Past tense**

Where **were** you born?

  I **was** born in Argentina.

Were you born in Buenos Aires?

  Yes, I **was**.

  No, I **wasn't**. I **was** born in Córdoba.

When **did** you **move** to Los Angeles?

  I **moved** here 10 years ago. I **didn't speak** English.

Did you **take** English classes in Argentina?

  Yes, I **did**. I **took** classes for a year.

  No, I **didn't**. My aunt **taught** me at home.

GRAMMAR PLUS *see page 132*

A Complete these conversations. Then practice with a partner.

1. A: Your English is very good. When _____ you begin to study English?

  B: I _____ in middle school.

  A: What _____ you think of English class at first?

  B: I _____ it was a little difficult, but fun.

2. A: Where _____ you born?

  B: I _____ born in Mexico.

  A: _____ you grow up there?

  B: No, I _____ . I _____ up in Canada.

3. A: Where _____ you meet your best friend?

  B: We _____ in high school.

  A: Do you still see each other?

  B: Yes, but not very often. She _____ to South Korea two years ago.

4. A: _____ you have a favorite teacher when you _____ a child?

  B: Yes, I _____ . I _____ a very good teacher named Mr. Potter.

  A: What _____ he teach?

  B: He _____ math.

B **PAIR WORK** Take turns asking the questions in part A. Give your own information when answering.

4 LISTENING Why did you move?

▶ **A** Listen to interviews with two immigrants to the United States. Why did they move to the U.S.A.?

▶ **B** Listen again and complete the chart.

	Enrique	**Jessica**
1. What were the most difficult changes?		
2. What do they miss the most?		

C **GROUP WORK** Enrique and Jessica talk about difficult changes. What could be some positive things about moving to a city like New York?

5 SPEAKING Tell me about yourself.

A **PAIR WORK** Check (✓) six questions below and add your own questions.
Then interview a classmate you don't know very well. Ask follow-up questions.

- ☐ Where were your grandparents born?
- ☐ Where did they grow up?
- ☐ Did you see them a lot when you were young?
- ☐ Who's your favorite relative?
- ☐ When did you first study English?
- ☐ Can you speak other languages?
- ☐ What were your best subjects in middle school?
- ☐ What subjects didn't you like?

_____

A: Where were your grandparents born?
B: My grandfather was born in Brazil,
 but my grandmother was born in Colombia.
A: Really? Where did they first meet?

useful expressions
Oh, that's interesting. Really? Me, too! Wow! Tell me more.

B **GROUP WORK** Tell the group what you learned about your partner. Then answer any questions.

"Vera's grandfather was born in Brazil, but her grandmother was born in . . ."

6 WORD POWER

A Complete the word map. Add two more words of your own to each category.
Then compare with a partner.

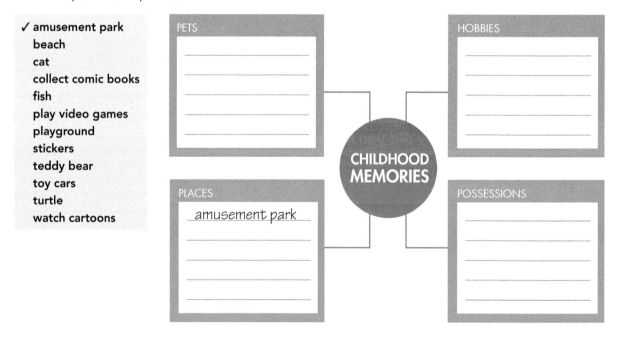

✓ amusement park
beach
cat
collect comic books
fish
play video games
playground
stickers
teddy bear
toy cars
turtle
watch cartoons

PETS

HOBBIES

CHILDHOOD MEMORIES

PLACES
  amusement park

POSSESSIONS

B **PAIR WORK** Choose three words from the word map and use them
to describe some of your childhood memories.

A: I loved to watch cartoons when I was a kid.
B: Me, too. What was your favorite?
A: I liked anything with superheroes in it. What about you?

A Listen to these statements about changes. Check (✓) those that are true about you.

☐ **1.** "When I was a kid, I never used to play sports, but now I like to keep fit."

☐ **2.** "I used to go out with friends a lot, but now I don't have any free time."

☐ **3.** "When I was younger, I didn't use to collect anything, but now I do."

☐ **4.** "I didn't use to be a good student, but now I love to study and learn new things."

☐ **5.** "I never used to follow politics, but now I read the news online every morning."

☐ **6.** "I used to be really neat and organized, but now I'm very messy."

☐ **7.** "I used to care a lot about my appearance. Now, I'm too busy to care about how I look."

B **PAIR WORK** Look at the statements again. Which changes are positive? Which are negative?

"I think the first one is a positive change. It's good to exercise."

8 GRAMMAR FOCUS

> ### Used to
>
> **Used to** refers to something that you regularly did in the past but don't do anymore.
>
> **Did** you **use to** collect things?
>
> Yes, I **used to** collect comic books.
>
> No, I **didn't use to** collect anything, but now I collect old records.
>
> What sports **did** you **use to** play?
>
> I **used to play** baseball and volleyball.
>
> I **never used to** play sports, but now I play tennis.
>
> GRAMMAR PLUS *see page 132*

A Complete these questions and answers. Then compare with a partner.

1. A: _____Did_____ you _____use to_____ have any pets when you were a kid?

B: Yes, I _____ have a white cat named Snowball.

2. A: _____ you and your classmates _____ play together after school?

B: No, we _____ play during the week. We _____ study a lot.

3. A: What music _____ you _____ listen to?

B: I _____ listen to rock a lot. Actually, I still do.

4. A: What hobbies _____ you _____ have when you were little?

B: I _____ have any hobbies, but now I play chess every week.

B How have you changed? Write sentences about yourself using *used to* or *didn't use to*. Then compare with a partner. Who has changed the most?

your hairstyle   your taste in music
your hobbies   the way you dress

I used to wear my hair much longer.
I didn't use to have a beard.

9 PRONUNCIATION *Used to*

▶ **A** Listen and practice. Notice that the pronunciation of *used to* and *use to* is the same.

When I was a child, I **used to** play the guitar.
 I **used to** have a nickname.
 I didn't **use to** like scary movies.
 I didn't **use to** study very hard at school.

B **PAIR WORK** Practice the sentences you wrote in Exercise 8, part B. Pay attention to the pronunciation of *used to* and *use to*.

10 SPEAKING Memories

A **PAIR WORK** Add three questions to this list. Then take turns asking and answering the questions. Ask follow-up questions.

1. What's your favorite childhood memory?
2. What sports or games did you use to play when you were younger?
3. Did you use to have a nickname?
4. Where did you use to spend your vacations?
5. Is your taste in food different now?
6. _____
7. _____
8. _____

B **CLASS ACTIVITY** Tell the class two interesting things about your partner.

11 WRITING We used to have a lot of fun.

A Write a paragraph about things you used to do as a child. Use some of your ideas from Exercise 10.

> I grew up in a small town, and my friends and I used to play outside a lot. We used to play all kinds of games. My favorite was hide-and-seek. We also used to ride our bikes to a beautiful lake near our school . . .

B **GROUP WORK** Share your paragraphs and answer any questions. Did you and your classmates use to do the same things? Do kids today do the same things you used to do?

12 INTERCHANGE 1 We have a lot in common.

Find out more about your classmates. Go to Interchange 1 on page 114.

A Scan the article. Where was Kahlo from? What happened when she was 18? Who did she marry?

A Life in Paintings:
The Frida Kahlo Story

Mexican painter Frida Kahlo (1907–1954) was both a talented artist and a woman of great courage. Her paintings tell an amazing story of tragedy and hope.

At the age of six, Kahlo developed polio, and she spent nine months in bed. The illness damaged her right leg forever. Most girls didn't use to play sports back then, but Kahlo played soccer and took up boxing. Exercising helped Kahlo get stronger. Kahlo even dreamed of becoming a doctor one day.

At 18, Kahlo was in a terrible bus crash, and her destiny changed. She wore a full body cast for months because her injuries were so bad. But again, Kahlo refused to give up. She entertained herself by painting self-portraits. She said, "I paint myself because I'm often alone, and because I am the subject I know best."

Kahlo suffered from very bad health the rest of her life, but she continued to paint. Other artists began to recognize her talent – an unusual achievement for a woman at the time. In 1929, she married famous Mexican painter Diego Rivera, but their marriage was troubled. Kahlo once said, "There have been two great accidents in my life . . . Diego was by far the worst."

Kahlo became pregnant three times. Unfortunately, because of her injuries from the bus accident and her generally poor health, none of her babies survived childbirth. This sadness almost destroyed Kahlo. Her paintings often show a broken woman, both in heart and body.

When she traveled, Kahlo always attracted attention. She dressed in long traditional Mexican skirts, wore her hair in long braids, and let her thick eyebrows grow naturally. She chose to look different, and people noticed her beauty everywhere she went.

Kahlo died at the age of 47 in the house where she was born. Her life was short, but extraordinary. Her paintings still amaze people with their honesty and originality.

B Read the article. Then circle the following words in the article and match them to the definitions below.

1. courage _____
2. tragedy _____
3. destiny _____
4. cast _____
5. recognize _____
6. injury _____

a. ability to control your fear in a difficult situation
b. accept that something is good or valuable
c. damage to a person's body
d. a special hard case that protects a broken bone
e. the things that will happen in the future
f. very sad event or situation

C Answer the questions.

1. What did Kahlo do to get healthier after her childhood illness?
2. Why did Kahlo start painting?
3. Why did Kahlo often do self-portraits?
4. What did Kahlo compare her marriage to?
5. Why couldn't Kahlo have children?
6. What was unusual about Kahlo's appearance?

D GROUP WORK What was unusual about Kahlo's life?
When do you think it's good to be different from what people expect?

2 Life in the city

▶ Discuss transportation and public services
▶ Ask questions about visiting cities

1 WORD POWER Compound nouns

A Match the words in columns A and B to make compound nouns.
(More than one combination may be possible.)

subway + station = subway station

A	B
bicycle	center
bus	garage
green	jam
parking	lane
recycling	light
street	space
subway	stand
taxi	station
traffic	stop
train	system

traffic jam

green space

B **PAIR WORK** Which of these things can you find where you live?

A: There are a lot of bus lanes.   **B:** Yes. But there isn't a subway system.

2 PERSPECTIVES City services

A Listen to these opinions about city services. Match them to the correct pictures.

YOUR VOICE COUNTS!

_____ 1. The streets are dark and dangerous.
I don't think there are enough police officers.
And we need more streetlights.

_____ 2. There's too much pollution from cars,
motorcycles, and old buses. In cities with less
pollution, people are healthier.

_____ 3. There should be fewer cars, but I think
that the biggest problem is parking. There just
isn't enough parking.

B **PAIR WORK** Does your city or town have similar problems?
What do you think is the biggest problem?

3 GRAMMAR FOCUS

▶ Expressions of quantity

With count nouns	With noncount nouns
There are **too many** cars.	There is **too much** pollution.
There should be **fewer** cars.	There should be **less** pollution.
We need **more** streetlights.	We need **more** public transportation.
There aren't **enough** police officers.	There isn't **enough** parking.

GRAMMAR PLUS *see page 133*

A Complete these statements about city problems. Then compare with a partner. (More than one answer may be possible.)

1. We need _____ public schools.
2. There are _____ accidents.
3. There are _____ public parks.
4. There is _____ noise all the time.
5. There is _____ recycling in our city.
6. The government should build _____ affordable housing.
7. The city needs _____ bicycle lanes.
8. There are _____ free Wi-Fi hotspots.

B **PAIR WORK** Write sentences about the city or town you are living in. Then compare with another pair.

1. The city should provide more . . .
2. We have too many . . .
3. There's too much . . .
4. There isn't enough . . .
5. There should be fewer . . .
6. We don't have enough . . .
7. There should be less . . .
8. We need more . . .

4 LISTENING It'll take forever.

▶ **A** Listen to a city resident talk to her new neighbor about the city. Check (✓) True or False for each statement.

	True	False	
1. Jacob already started his new job downtown.	☐	✓	*He starts his new job tomorrow.*
2. The city needs more buses.	☐	☐	
3. There aren't enough tourists in the city.	☐	☐	
4. Not many people ride bikes in the city.	☐	☐	
5. Sophia offers to lend Jacob her bike.	☐	☐	

▶ **B** Listen again. For the false statements, write the correct information.

C **PAIR WORK** What things can a city do to improve the problems that Sophia mentions? Does your city have similar problems?

5 DISCUSSION Rate your city.

A GROUP WORK Which of these services are available in your city or town? Discuss what is good and bad about each one.

_____ recycling system   _____ parks and green spaces   _____ affordable housing
_____ transportation system   _____ Wi-Fi service   _____ recreational and sports facilities

B GROUP WORK How would you rate the services where you live? Give each item a rating from 1 to 5.

1 = terrible   2 = needs improvement   3 = average   4 = good   5 = excellent

A: I'd give the parks a 4. There are enough parks, but they aren't always clean.

B: I think a rating of 4 is too high. There aren't enough green spaces in many areas of the city . . .

6 WRITING A social media post

A Read this post about traffic in the city on a social networking page.

B Use your statements from Exercise 3, part B, and any new ideas to write a post about a local issue.

C GROUP WORK Take turns reading your messages. Do you have any of the same concerns?

> Posted by Michelle K
> Today at 5:30
>
> I'm tired of this city. There's too much traffic, and it's getting worse. It used to take me 15 minutes to get to class. Today it took me more than 30 minutes during rush hour! There should be more subway lines. I think people want to use public transportation, but we need more . . .
>
> comment

7 SNAPSHOT

Common Tourist Questions

- [ ] What's the best way to see the city?
- [ ] How much do taxis cost?
- [ ] Which hotel is closest to the airport?
- [ ] Where should I go shopping?
- [ ] What festivals or events are taking place?
- [ ] Where can I buy a SIM card for my phone?
- [ ] Where's a good place to meet friends?
- [ ] Where can I get a city guide?
- [ ] What museums should I see?
- [ ] What are some family-friendly activities?

Check (✓) the questions you can answer about your city.
What other questions could a visitor ask about your city?
Talk to your classmates. Find answers to the questions you didn't check.

8 CONVERSATION Do you know where . . . ?

▶ **A** Listen and practice.

Rachel: Excuse me. Do you know where the nearest ATM is?

Clerk: There's one down the street, across from the café.

Rachel: Great. And do you know where I can catch a bus downtown?

Clerk: Sure. Just look for the signs for "Public Transportation."

Rachel: OK. And can you tell me how often they run?

Clerk: They run every 10 minutes or so.

Rachel: And just one more thing. Could you tell me where the restrooms are?

Clerk: Right inside. Do you see where that sign is?

Rachel: Oh. Thanks a lot.

▶ **B** Listen to the rest of the conversation. Check (✓) the information that Rachel asks for.

☐ the cost of the bus fare
☐ the cost of a city guide
☐ the location of a taxi stand
☐ the location of a bookstore

9 GRAMMAR FOCUS

▶ **Indirect questions from Wh-questions**

Wh-questions with *be*	Indirect questions
Where is the nearest ATM?	Could you tell me **where the nearest ATM is**?
Where are the restrooms?	Do you know **where the restrooms are**?
Wh-questions with *do*	**Indirect questions**
How often do the buses run?	Can you tell me **how often the buses run**?
What time does the bookstore open?	Do you know **what time the bookstore opens**?
Wh-questions with *can*	**Indirect questions**
Where can I catch the bus?	Do you know **where I can catch the bus**?

GRAMMAR PLUS *see page 133*

A Write indirect questions using these Wh-questions. Then compare with a partner.

1. Where can I rent a car?
2. How much does a city tour cost?
3. How early do the stores open?
4. Where's the nearest Wi-Fi hotspot?
5. How much does a taxi to the airport cost?
6. What time does the post office open?
7. Where's an inexpensive hotel in this area?
8. How late do the nightclubs stay open?

B PAIR WORK Take turns asking and answering the questions you wrote in part A.

A: Do you know where I can rent a car?
B: You can rent one at the airport.

10 PRONUNCIATION Syllable stress

▶ **A** Listen and practice. Notice which syllable has the main stress in these two-syllable words.

● ●   ● ●
subway   garage
traffic   police

▶ **B** Listen to the stress in these words. Write them in the correct columns. Then compare with a partner.

		● ●	● ●
buses	improve	_____	_____
bookstore	provide	_____	_____
event	public	_____	_____
hotel	taxis	_____	_____

11 SPEAKING The best of our town

A Complete the chart with indirect questions.

	Name:
1. Where's the best area to stay? "Do you know where the best area to stay is ?"	
2. What's the best way to see the city? " ?"	
3. How late do the buses run? " ?"	
4. How much do people tip in a restaurant? " ?"	
5. What's a good restaurant to try the local food? " ?"	
6. What are the most popular attractions? " ?"	
7. Where can I hear live music? " ?"	

B PAIR WORK Use the indirect questions in the chart to interview a classmate about the city or town where you live. Take notes.

A: Do you know where the best area to stay is?
B: It depends. You can stay near . . .

C CLASS ACTIVITY Share your answers with the class. Who knows the most about your city or town?

12 INTERCHANGE 2 Top travel destinations

Discuss ways to attract tourists to a city. Go to Interchange 2 on page 115.

A Skim the article. Which of the following things does it mention?

transportation   natural areas   safety   entertainment   schools   housing

---

The World's Happiest Cities ☺

Search 🔍

Home   About   Articles   Community   *Traveling*   Food   Booking

When author Dan Buettner went looking for the world's happiest people on four different continents, he found some really great places to live!

_____ a. Singapore

With a population of 5.1 million, Singapore is really crowded, and people work very long hours. Yet 95 percent of Singapore residents say they are happy. Subway trains almost always arrive on time. The police are good at their jobs and always ready to help. People in Singapore love that their city is so clean and safe.

_____ b. Aarhus, Denmark

Although people pay an incredible 68 percent of their salaries in taxes here, they get lots of services for free: healthcare, education, and daycare for young children. The city has lots of entertainment options too, like museums, shopping, and nightlife. For those who love nature, it's only a 15-minute bike ride to incredible beaches and forests.

_____ c. San Luis Obispo, California, U.S.A.

People here smile and feel happy more than in any other American city. Most people travel less than 10 minutes to work, and there are lots of bike lanes, so commuting is easy. Residents share their joy with others, too. Almost 25 percent of people in San Luis Obispo volunteer to help people in their free time.

_____ d. Monterrey, Mexico

Although many of its people don't earn high salaries, they still feel rich. People in Monterrey have strong family relationships and very busy social lives. They also have a positive attitude about life – they laugh and stay strong even in times of trouble.

Adapted from http://www.rd.com/advice/travel/the-4-happiest-cities-on-earth

---

B Read the article. Match the paragraphs (a–d) to the pictures (1–4).

C Read the comments from residents of these four cities. Which city do you think they live in? Write the letter.

1. "I spend a lot of time with my relatives." _____
2. "A lot of what I earn goes to the government, but I don't mind." _____
3. "I can see great art in my city." _____
4. "I often have to spend eleven hours or more in the office." _____
5. "I help children with their homework after school for free." _____
6. "I try to be cheerful, even when things are going badly." _____
7. "I take the train to work, and I'm never late." _____
8. "On weekends, I can get out of the city without taking the car." _____

D **PAIR WORK** Which sentences in part C are true for you and your city or town? How would you improve the place where you live?

Units 1–2 Progress check

SELF-ASSESSMENT

How well can you do these things? Check (✓) the boxes.

I can . . .	Very well	OK	A little
Understand descriptions of childhood (Ex. 1)	☐	☐	☐
Ask and answer questions about childhood and past times (Ex. 1, 2)	☐	☐	☐
Express opinions about cities and towns; agree and disagree (Ex. 3)	☐	☐	☐
Ask for and give information about a city or town (Ex. 4)	☐	☐	☐

1 LISTENING What was that like?

▶ **A** Listen to an interview with Charlotte, a fashion designer. Answer the questions in complete sentences.

1. Where did she grow up? What is her hometown like? _____
2. What did she want to do when she grew up? _____
3. What were her hobbies as a child? _____
4. What sport did she use to play? _____
5. What was her favorite place? What did she use to do there? _____

B **PAIR WORK** Use the questions in part A to interview a partner about his or her childhood. Ask follow-up questions to get more information.

2 DISCUSSION In the past, . . .

A **PAIR WORK** Talk about how life in your country has changed in the last 50 years. Ask questions like these:

What kinds of homes did people live in?
How did people use to communicate?
What did people use to do in their free time?
How did people use to dress?
How were schools different?
What kinds of jobs did men have? women?

A: What kinds of homes did people live in?
B: Houses used to be bigger. Now most people live in small apartments.

B **GROUP WORK** Compare your answers. Do you think life was better in the past? Why or why not?

3 SURVEY Are there enough parks?

A What do you think about these things in your city or town? Complete the survey.

	Not enough	OK	Too many/Too much
free shows and concerts	☐	☐	☐
places to go dancing	☐	☐	☐
parks and green spaces	☐	☐	☐
places to go shopping	☐	☐	☐
noise	☐	☐	☐
places to sit and have coffee	☐	☐	☐
public transportation	☐	☐	☐
places to meet new people	☐	☐	☐

B **GROUP WORK** Compare your opinions and suggest ways to make
your city or town better. Then agree on three improvements.

A: How would you make our city better?

B: There should be more shows and concerts. There aren't enough free activities for young people.

C: I disagree. There should be more schools. We don't need more entertainment.

4 ROLE PLAY Can I help you?

Student A: Imagine you are a visitor in your city or town.
Write five indirect questions about these
categories. Then ask your questions to the
hotel front-desk clerk.

Transportation   Sightseeing
Hotels   Shopping
Restaurants   Entertainment

Student B: You are a hotel front-desk clerk. Answer
the guest's questions.

A: Excuse me.

B: Can I help you?

Change roles and try the role play again.

useful expressions
Let me think. Oh, yes, . . .
I'm not really sure, but I think . . .
Sorry, I don't know.

WHAT'S NEXT?

Look at your Self-assessment again. Do you need to review anything?

3 Making changes

▶ Compare houses and apartments
▶ Discuss life changes

1 WORD POWER Homes

A These words are used to describe houses and apartments. Which are positive (**P**)? Which are negative (**N**)?

bright	_____	dingy	_____	private	_____
comfortable	_____	expensive	_____	quiet	_____
convenient	_____	huge	_____	run-down	_____
cramped	_____	inconvenient	_____	safe	_____
dangerous	_____	modern	_____	small	_____
dark	_____	noisy	_____	spacious	_____

cramped

B **PAIR WORK** Tell your partner two positive and two negative features of your house or apartment.

"I live in a nice neighborhood. It's safe and very convenient. However, the apartment is a little cramped and kind of expensive."

2 PERSPECTIVES How's your new apartment?

A Listen to a family talk about their new apartment. Which opinions are about the building or the neighborhood? Which are about the apartment?

1. I don't like living in an apartment. We don't have as much privacy as we had in our old place.

2. I just can't sleep at night. The neighbors make too much noise. The building isn't as quiet as our old one.

3. The new apartment is too dark and too hot. There aren't enough windows.

4. Our new apartment isn't big enough for our family. We don't have a big kitchen anymore, so cooking is difficult.

5. The location is just as convenient as the old one, but there aren't as many good restaurants around.

B **PAIR WORK** Look at the opinions again. Talk about similar problems you have.

A: My next-door neighbors make too much noise. They have parties every Saturday.
B: My brother has the same problem. His neighbor's band practices all weekend!

3 GRAMMAR FOCUS

▶ **Evaluations and comparisons**

Evaluations with adjectives

Our apartment is**n't** big **enough** for our family.

This apartment is **too** hot.

Comparisons with adjectives

The building is**n't as** quiet **as** our old one.

The location is **just as** convenient **as** the old one.

Evaluations with nouns

There are**n't enough** windows.

The neighbors make **too much** noise.

Comparisons with nouns

We do**n't** have **as many** bedrooms **as** we used to.

We do**n't** have **as much** privacy **as** we had.

GRAMMAR PLUS *see page 134*

A Imagine you are looking for a house or an apartment to rent. Read the two ads. Then rewrite the opinions using the words in parentheses. Compare with a partner.

For rent

Spacious, modern house ⌂

3 bedrooms, 1 bathroom; in quiet suburb 20 miles from downtown; 2-car garage; $1500 per month.

For rent

Comfortable apartment

2 bedrooms, 1 bathroom; downtown, near subway; 1 parking space; built in 1920; $900 per month.

1. The house is 20 miles from downtown. (too)
2. It's not convenient enough. (too)
3. It has only one bathroom. (not enough)
4. The rent is very high. (too)

5. The apartment is too old. (not enough)
6. There are only two bedrooms. (not enough)
7. It's not spacious enough. (too)
8. There's only one parking space. (not enough)

It's too far from downtown.

B Write comparisons of the house and the apartment using these words and *as . . . as*. Then compare with a partner.

big	noisy
bedrooms	expensive
bathrooms	modern
spacious	convenient
private	parking spaces

The apartment isn't as big as the house.

The apartment doesn't have as many bedrooms as the house.

C **GROUP WORK** Which would you prefer to rent: the house or the apartment? Why?

A: I'd choose the apartment. The house isn't close enough to public transportation.

B: I'd rent the house because the apartment is too small.

4 PRONUNCIATION Unpronounced vowels

▶ **A** Listen and practice. The vowel immediately after a stressed syllable is sometimes not pronounced.

● ●   ● ● ●

average   comfortable
different   interesting
separate   vegetable

B Write four sentences using some of the words in part A. Then read them with a partner. Pay attention to unpronounced vowels.

> *Today, the average house is much smaller than 50 years ago.*

5 LISTENING A home away from home

▶ **A** Listen to Josh describe a "capsule hotel." Check (✓) True or False for each statement.

	True	False	
1. Tokyo sometimes feels too noisy.	☐	✓	*Sometimes it feels too big.*
2. A capsule hotel is not as convenient as a regular hotel.	☐	☐	
3. Inside every capsule there is a TV, a radio, and an alarm clock.	☐	☐	
4. The capsule is a good option if you're busy and tired.	☐	☐	
5. Josh would recommend a capsule hotel to anyone.	☐	☐	

▶ **B** Listen again. For the false statements, write the correct information.

C GROUP WORK Where else do you think a capsule hotel would be popular? Why?

6 WRITING My new home

A Imagine you've just moved to this apartment. Write an email to a friend comparing your old home to your new one.

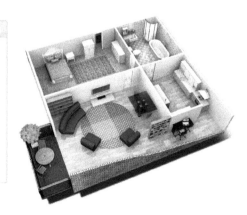

● ● ● ‹ ›   Reply   Forward

Hi Chloe,
How's everything? I have some great news. We just moved to a new apartment! Do you remember our old apartment? It was too small, and I didn't have enough space for my things. My new bedroom is spacious, and I have a separate area to study in. The apartment also has a balcony. It isn't very big, but now we can have breakfast outdoors on Sundays. The . . .

B PAIR WORK Read each other's emails. How are your descriptions similar? different?

7 SNAPSHOT

MAKE A WISH

- ☐ Have a healthier lifestyle
- ☐ Go back to school
- ☐ Start my own business
- ☐ Improve my personality
- ☐ Enjoy life more
- ☐ Move to a new home
- ☐ Add more hours to the day
- ☐ Make new friends
- ☐ Do volunteer work
- ☐ Spend more time with my family

Check (✓) some of the things you would like to do. Then tell a partner why.
Which of these wishes would be easy to achieve? Which would be difficult or impossible?
What other things would you like to change about your life? Why?

8 CONVERSATION I wish I could.

▶ **A** Listen and practice.

Harry: So, are you still living with your parents, Dylan?

Dylan: Yes, I am. But sometimes I wish I had my own apartment.

Harry: Why? Don't you like living at home?

Dylan: It's OK, but my parents are always asking me to come home early. I wish they'd stop worrying about me.

Harry: Yeah, parents are like that!

Dylan: Plus, they don't like my friends, and they won't stop criticizing them. I wish life weren't so difficult.

Harry: So, why don't you move out?

Dylan: Hey, I wish I could, but where else can I get free room and board?

▶ **B** Listen to the rest of the conversation. What changes would Harry like to make in his life?

9 GRAMMAR FOCUS

▶ *Wish*

Use *wish* + past tense to refer to present wishes.

I **live** with my parents.	Life **is** difficult.
I wish I **didn't live** with my parents.	I wish it **were*** easier.
I wish I **had** my own apartment.	I wish it **weren't** so difficult.
I **can't move** out.	My parents **won't stop** worrying about me.
I wish I **could move** out.	I wish they **would stop** worrying about me.

*For the verb *be*, *were* is used with all pronouns after *wish*.

GRAMMAR PLUS *see page 134*

A Read these other comments that Dylan makes. Then rewrite the sentences using *wish*. (More than one answer is possible.)

1. My mother doesn't like my girlfriend.   *I wish she liked my girlfriend.*
2. My girlfriend is too short to be a model.   *She wishes she were taller.*
3. My classes are really boring.   _____
4. I'm not on vacation right now.   _____
5. My family can't afford a bigger house.   _____
6. The neighbors won't stop making noise.   _____
7. Harry doesn't like his job.   _____

B **PAIR WORK** Think of five things you wish you could change. Then discuss them with your partner.

A: What do you wish you could change?

B: Well, I don't have much free time. I wish I had time to . . .

10 SPEAKING   Make it happen.

A If you could wish for three things, what would they be? Write down your wishes.

B **GROUP WORK** How can you make your wishes come true? Get suggestions from your classmates.

A: I wish I had more money.

B: Why don't you look for another job?

A: I don't have enough experience. I wish I had a diploma.

C: You can go back to school or take an online course.

11 INTERCHANGE 3   A dream come true

Find out more about your classmates' wishes. Go to Interchange 3 on page 116.

A Skim the article. Which of these sentences is true?

Boyle decided that a life without money was impossible to live.

Boyle wanted to give people the chance to live a different lifestyle.

THE MAN WITH NO MONEY

A Can you imagine your life without any money? Not even a cent, a real, or a peso? One man decided to try it out.

B Mark Boyle was a successful manager of an organic food company in Ireland. He had a good life. But he worried about the damage humans were doing to the environment. He also believed people bought more things than they needed. Boyle wished we grew our own food and made our own furniture, so we wouldn't waste as much as we do today. So one day, he left his job and started an experiment – could he live for a year without buying anything?

C He sold his houseboat and moved into an old mobile home. He got it for free from a website where people give away things they don't want. It wasn't as comfortable as his old place at first, but he soon made it feel like home. He parked it on a farm near Bristol, England. Instead of paying rent, he worked on the farm. He burned wood from the forest to heat his home, so he didn't pay electricity or gas bills.

D Boyle didn't go shopping, either. He grew his own fruit and vegetables. He also looked for food in the trash cans of supermarkets and cooked it on a wood stove. He made his own toothpaste from fish bones and seeds. To wash his clothes, he used a special type of nut to make soap. Boyle even built his own toilet and used old newspapers from the farm for toilet paper.

E He began using money again after eighteen months. He says his life change made him feel healthier, happier, and closer to nature. He wrote two books about his experience and used the money to start "The Free House," a farm in Ireland where people can live without money.

B Read the article. Then circle the correct word or words.

1. Before the experiment, Mark Boyle was **good at / unhappy with** his job.
2. Boyle thought that people **spent too much / discussed money too often**.
3. Boyle worked on a farm **to earn money to pay rent / so he didn't have to pay rent**.
4. Boyle made cleaning products from things he found in **trash cans / the forest**.
5. Boyle generally felt **worse / better** after living without money.

C Match the sentences to the paragraphs they describe. Write the letter.

____ 1. Describes a big change that happened in the person's life
____ 2. Describes the way the person's everyday habits changed
____ 3. Asks a question to make the reader think about the topic
____ 4. Gives general information about the past of the main person in the story
____ 5. Explains how the person felt about the whole experiment

D **PAIR WORK** Discuss Boyle's experience. Would you like to try it?

Do you think people today spend too much money on things they don't need?

4 Have you ever tried it?

▶ Describe past personal experiences
▶ Discuss food, recipes, and cooking methods

1 SNAPSHOT

TRADITIONAL DISHES FROM AROUND THE WORLD

Lebanon	South Korea	Singapore	Brazil
Kibbeh Labanieh	**Galbi**	**Gulai Kepala Ikan**	**Moqueca**
Lamb or beef meatballs cooked in yogurt with spices	Korean-style barbecued meat	A dish made from a fish head cooked in a rich curry sauce	Fish and shellfish stew cooked in coconut milk in a clay pot

Which dishes are made with meat? with fish?
Have you ever tried any of these dishes? Which ones would you like to try?
What traditional foods are popular in your country?

2 CONVERSATION   I've never heard of that!

▶ **A** Listen and practice.

Aiden Hey, this sounds strange – frog legs with butter and garlic sauce. Have you ever eaten frog legs?

Claire Yes, I have. I had them here just last week.

Aiden Did you like them?

Claire Yes, I did. They were delicious! Why don't you try some?

Aiden No, I don't think so. I'm a little scared of them.

Server Have you decided on an appetizer yet?

Claire Yes. I'll have a small order of frog legs, please.

Server And you, sir?

Aiden I think I'll have the snails.

Claire Snails? That's adventurous of you!

▶ **B** Listen to the rest of the conversation. How did Aiden like the snails? What else did he order?

3 PRONUNCIATION Consonant clusters

▶ A Listen and practice. Notice how the two consonants at the beginning of a word are pronounced together.

/k/	/t/	/m/	/n/	/p/	/r/	/l/
scan	start	smart	snack	spare	brown	blue
skim	step	smile	snow	speak	gray	play

B **PAIR WORK** Find one more word on page 22 for each consonant cluster in part A. Then practice saying the words.

4 GRAMMAR FOCUS

▶ **Simple past vs. present perfect**

Use the simple past for experiences at a definite time in the past.
Use the present perfect for experiences within a time period up to the present.

Have you ever **eaten** frog legs?	**Have** you ever **been** to a Vietnamese restaurant?
Yes, I **have**. I **tried** them last month.	No, I **haven't**. But I **ate** at a Thai restaurant last night.
Did you **like** them?	**Did** you **go** alone?
Yes, I **did**. They **were** delicious.	No, I **went** with some friends.

GRAMMAR PLUS see page 135

A Complete these conversations. Then practice with a partner.

1. **A:** Have you ever _____eaten_____ (eat) sushi?
   B: Yes, I _____. In fact, I _____ (eat) some just last week.
2. **A:** Have you ever _____ (try) Moroccan food?
   B: No, I _____, but I'd like to.
3. **A:** Did you _____ (have) breakfast today?
   B: Yes, I _____. I _____ (eat) a huge breakfast.
4. **A:** Have you ever _____ (be) to a picnic at the beach?
   B: Yes, I _____. My family and I _____ (have) a picnic on the beach last month. We _____ (cook) hamburgers.
5. **A:** Did you _____ (cook) dinner last night?
   B: Yes, I _____. I _____ (make) spaghetti with tomato sauce.

B **PAIR WORK** Ask and answer the questions in part A. Give your own information.

5 LISTENING Have you tried this before?

▶ A Listen to six people ask questions in a restaurant. Are they talking about these items? Write **Y** (yes) or **N** (no).

1. _N_ plate
   juice
2. ___ the check

3. ___ cake

4. ___ meat

5. ___ water

6. ___ the menu

▶ B Listen again. For the no (**N**) items, write what they might be talking about instead.

6 SPEAKING How did you like it?

PAIR WORK Ask your partner these questions and four more of your own.
Then ask follow-up questions.

Have you ever drunk fresh sugar cane juice?
Have you ever been to a vegetarian restaurant?
Have you ever had an unusual ice cream flavor?
Have you ever eaten something you didn't like?

A: Have you ever drunk fresh sugar cane juice?
B: Yes, I have. I drank it in Egypt once.
A: How did you like it?
B: I loved it, actually.

7 INTERCHANGE 4 Oh, really?

Find out some interesting facts about your classmates. Go to Interchange 4 on page 117.

8 WORD POWER Cooking methods

A How do you cook the foods below? Check (✓) the methods that are most common.

| bake | boil | fry | grill | roast | steam |

Methods / Foods	fish	shrimp	eggs	chicken	beef	potatoes	onions	corn	bananas
bake	☐	☐	☐	☐	☐	☐	☐	☐	☐
boil	☐	☐	☐	☐	☐	☐	☐	☐	☐
fry	☐	☐	☐	☐	☐	☐	☐	☐	☐
grill	☐	☐	☐	☐	☐	☐	☐	☐	☐
roast	☐	☐	☐	☐	☐	☐	☐	☐	☐
steam	☐	☐	☐	☐	☐	☐	☐	☐	☐

B **PAIR WORK** What's your favorite way to cook or eat the foods in part A?

A: Have you ever fried bananas?
B: No, I haven't. But sometimes I grill them.

9 PERSPECTIVES Comfort food

▶ **A** Listen to this recipe for macaroni and cheese. Do you think this is a healthy dish?

Baked Macaroni and Cheese

- 1 package elbow macaroni
- 4 tablespoons butter
- 2 cups heavy cream
- 4 cups cheddar cheese, shredded

First, boil the macaroni in a large pot for 5 minutes.
Then melt the butter on medium heat and add the cream.
Stir for about 2 minutes. Next, add the cheese. Stir until the
cheese is melted. Season with salt and pepper.
After that, add the cooked macaroni and mix well. Finally,
bake for 20 minutes.

B **PAIR WORK** Look at the steps in the recipe again. Number the pictures
from 1 to 5. Would you like to try this traditional American dish?

10 GRAMMAR FOCUS

▶ **Sequence adverbs**

First, boil the macaroni in a large pot.
Then melt the butter on medium heat.
Next, add the cheese.
After that, add the cooked macaroni.
Finally, bake for 20 minutes.

GRAMMAR PLUS *see page 135*

A Here's a recipe for a couscous salad. Look at the pictures and
number the steps from 1 to 5. Then add a sequence adverb
to each step.

☐ _____ drain the couscous and let it cool.

1 First, _____ chop some olives, parsley, and cheese.

☐ _____ toss the cooked couscous with the olives,
parsley, and cheese.

☐ _____ pour some couscous into the hot water and
let it sit for 10 minutes.

☐ _____ boil a pot of water.

B **PAIR WORK** Cover the recipe and look only at the pictures.
Explain each step of the recipe to your partner.

11 LISTENING How do you make it?

A Listen to people explain how to make these snacks. Which snack are they talking about? Number the photos from 1 to 4. (There is one extra photo.)

spaghetti   chocolate chip cookies   salsa   French toast   popcorn

B Listen again. Check (✓) the steps you hear for each recipe.

1. ✓ add   **2.** ☐ cut   **3.** ☐ stir   **4.** ☐ mix
    ✓ chop   ☐ heat   ☐ cook   ☐ bake
    ☐ heat   ☐ pour   ☐ cover   ☐ mash

C PAIR WORK Tell your partner how to make one of the snacks above. Your partner will guess which snack it is.

12 SPEAKING It's my favorite food.

GROUP WORK Discuss these questions.

What's your favorite food?
Is it easy to make?
What's in it?
How often do you eat it?
Where do you usually eat it?
How healthy is it?

"My favorite food is pizza. It's not difficult to make. First, . . ."

13 WRITING My cookbook

A Read this recipe. Is this an easy recipe to make?

Guacamole

First, chop the tomato, onion, chili pepper, and cilantro. Then scoop out the flesh of the avocados and mash it with a fork. Next, squeeze the lime and mix the juice with the avocado. Finally, combine all the ingredients, mix well, and season with salt to taste.

1 tomato
half a red onion
3 avocados
1 lime
1 fresh green chili pepper
2 tablespoons cilantro

B Now think of something you know how to make. First, write down the things you need. Then describe how to make it.

C GROUP WORK Read and discuss each recipe. Then choose one to share with the class. Explain why you chose it.

A Scan the article. Which city does pizza come from? When did pizza arrive in New York? What do people in Japan like on their pizzas?

PIZZA:
The World's Favorite Food?

Food, and the way we eat it, is always changing. As society develops, we learn new ways of growing, processing, and cooking food. _[a]_ Also, when people travel to live in other countries, they take their knowledge of cooking with them. And food must fit modern lifestyles and local tastes, too. One food that has done this successfully is the pizza.

The pizza we recognize today first appeared in Italy in 1889. A famous baker from Naples made a special pizza for the Italian royal family. _[b]_ Queen Margherita loved the dish so much, the baker named it after her. Since then, this simple meal of bread, cheese, and tomato has traveled the world, and it has adapted to local cultures.

Pizza began its journey in the 1890s, when many Italians moved to New York in search of a better life. There they continued to make pizzas, and the first pizzeria opened in 1905.

·LOMBARDI'S – 1905·

At first it was only popular with Italians, but by the late 1940s, Americans discovered a taste for it. Today, they spend an incredible $37 billion a year on pizzas. _[c]_

Pizza continued its travels around the world, adapting all the time. In Sweden, for example, it is not unusual to have peanuts and bananas on your pizza. _[d]_ Japan is a nation of seafood lovers, so not surprisingly, they love octopus and squid, as well as roasted seaweed, toppings. Australians sometimes choose kangaroo or crocodile, and in the Philippines they like mango on their pizza.

The popularity of the pizza is also related to our changing lifestyles. In today's super-fast society, people often don't have the time or energy to cook. So, they order takeout – and very often, it's a pizza. _[e]_ If you don't even have time to sit down, buy a single slice and eat it standing up!

The pizza has come a long way. From its beginnings in an Italian city, it has grown to become one of the world's favorite foods.

B Read the article. Where do these sentences belong? Write the letters a–e.

____ **1.** That's more than $100 per American!

____ **2.** What we ate 200 years ago was very different from what we eat today.

____ **3.** In Belgium, people eat chocolate pizzas with marshmallows on top.

____ **4.** Sometimes you don't even have to pick it up; it's delivered to your home.

____ **5.** He was very worried they wouldn't like it, but they did.

C How has local food changed in your country in the last 50 years? What new foods do you eat now that you didn't eat before?

Units 3–4 Progress check

SELF-ASSESSMENT

How well can you do these things? Check (✓) the boxes.

I can . . .	Very well	OK	A little
Evaluate a house or apartment (Ex. 1)	☐	☐	☐
Express opinions about houses or apartments; agree and disagree (Ex. 1)	☐	☐	☐
Discuss life changes (Ex. 2)	☐	☐	☐
Describe past personal experiences (Ex. 3)	☐	☐	☐
Describe recipes (Ex. 4)	☐	☐	☐

1 SPEAKING For rent

A PAIR WORK Use the topics in the box to write an ad for an apartment. Use this ad as a model. Make the apartment sound as good as possible.

FOR RENT
Comfortable 1-bedroom apartment
Spacious, bright; located downtown; convenient to public transportation; 1 bathroom, modern kitchen; 1-car garage

$1200 **a month**

age	windows	parking
size	bathroom(s)	cost
location	bedroom(s)	noise

B GROUP WORK Join another pair. Evaluate and compare the apartments. Which would you prefer to rent? Why?

A: There aren't enough bedrooms in your apartment.
B: But it's convenient.
C: Yes, but our apartment is just as convenient!

2 LISTENING Making changes

A Listen to three people talk about things they wish they could change. Check (✓) the topic each person is talking about.

1. ☐ city ☐ travel _____
2. ☐ school ☐ skills _____
3. ☐ free time ☐ money _____

B Listen again. Write one change each person would like to make.

C PAIR WORK Use the topics in part A to express your own wishes.

3 SURVEY Memorable meals

A Complete the survey with your food opinions and experiences.
Then use your information to write questions.

Me	Name
1. I've eaten _____. I liked it. <u>Have you ever eaten</u> ? <u>Did you like it</u> ?	
2. I've eaten _____. I hated it. _____? _____?	
3. I've never tried _____. But I want to. _____?	
4. I've been to the restaurant _____ I enjoyed it. _____?	
5. I've made _____ for my friends. They loved it. _____?	

B **CLASS ACTIVITY** Go around the class and ask
your questions. Find people who have had the
same experiences as you. Write a classmate's
name only once.

A: Have you ever eaten a sloppy joe sandwich?
B: Yes, I have.
A: Did you like it?
B: Yes . . . but it was too messy.

4 ROLE PLAY Reality cooking competition

GROUP WORK Work in groups of four. Two students
are the judges. Two students are the chefs.

Judges: Make a list of three ingredients for the chefs
to use. You will decide which chef creates the
best recipe.

Chefs: Think of a recipe using the three ingredients the
judges give you and other basic ingredients.
Name the recipe and describe how to make it.
"My recipe is called . . . . To make it, first . . . .
Then . . . . Next, ..."

Change roles and try the role play again.

WHAT'S NEXT?

Look at your Self-assessment again. Do you need to review anything?

5 Hit the road!

▶ Discuss vacation and travel plans
▶ Give travel advice

1 SNAPSHOT

What do you like to do on vacation?

take a fun trip | discover something new | stay home | enjoy nature

- ☐ visit a foreign country
- ☐ travel in my own country
- ☐ go to a music festival
- ☐ take a photography course
- ☐ hang out with friends
- ☐ host a family reunion
- ☐ go camping
- ☐ relax at the beach

Which activities do you like to do on vacation? Check (✓) the activities.
Which activities would you like to do on your next vacation?
Make a list of other activities you like to do on vacation. Then compare with a partner.

2 CONVERSATION I guess I'll just stay home.

▶ A Listen and practice.

Nora: I'm so excited! We have two weeks off! What are you going to do?

Lily: I'm not sure. I guess I'll just stay home. Maybe I'll hang out with some friends and watch my favorite series. What about you? Any plans?

Nora: Yeah, I'm going to relax at the beach with my cousin. We're going to go surfing every day. And my cousin likes to snorkel, so maybe we'll go snorkeling one day.

Lily: Sounds like fun.

Nora: Hey, why don't you come with us?

Lily: Do you mean it? I'd love to! I'll bring my surfboard!

Nora: That's great! The more the merrier!

▶ B Listen to the rest of the conversation. Where are they going to stay? How will they get there?

3 GRAMMAR FOCUS

▶ Future with *be going to* and *will*

Use *be going to* + verb for plans you've decided on.

What **are** you **going to do**?

I'm going to relax at the beach.

We**'re going to go** surfing every day.

I'm not **going to do** anything special.

Use *will* + verb for possible plans before you've made a decision.

What **are** you **going to do**?

I'm not sure. I **guess** I**'ll** just **stay** home.

Maybe I**'ll take** a course.

I don't know. I **think** I**'ll go** camping.

I **probably won't go** anywhere.

GRAMMAR PLUS *see page 136*

A Complete the conversation with appropriate forms of *be going to* or *will*. Then compare with a partner.

1. A: Have you made any vacation plans?

   B: Well, I've decided on one thing – I _____ take a bike tour.

   A: That's great! For how long?

   B: I _____ be away for about a week. I need to take some time off.

   A: So, when are you leaving?

   B: I'm not sure. I _____ probably leave around the end of next month.

   A: And where _____ you _____ go?

   B: I haven't thought about that yet. I guess I _____ go down south.

   A: That sounds like fun. _____ you _____ buy a new bicycle?

   B: I'm not sure. Actually, I probably _____ buy one – I don't have enough money right now. I guess I _____ rent one.

   A: _____ you _____ go with anyone?

   B: No. I need some time alone. I _____ travel by myself.

2. A: What are your plans for the holiday weekend?

   B: I _____ visit my parents.

   A: What _____ you _____ do there?

   B: Nothing much. I _____ hang out with some old school friends. And we _____ probably have a barbecue on Sunday.

   A: That sounds like fun. When _____ you _____ leave?

   B: I'm not sure yet. I _____ probably leave on Friday night if I don't need to work on Saturday.

   A: _____ you _____ fly there?

   B: I wish I could, but it's too expensive. I guess I _____ take the train.

   A: _____ you _____ go alone?

   B: Maybe my brother _____ go, too. He hasn't decided yet.

   A: Do you know when you are coming back?

   B: I think I _____ come back on Monday.

   A: Good. Then we can have dinner together on Monday.

B Have you thought about your next vacation? Write answers to these questions. (If you already have plans, use *be going to*. If you don't have fixed plans, use *will*.)

   1. How are you going to spend your next vacation?

   2. Where are you going to go?

   3. When are you going to take your vacation?

   4. How long are you going to be on vacation?

   5. Is anyone going to travel with you?

> I'm going to spend my next vacation . . .
>
> OR I'm not sure. Maybe I'll . . .

C GROUP WORK Take turns telling the group about your vacation plans. Use your information from part B.

4 WORD POWER Travel preparations

A Complete the chart. Then add one more word to each category.

ATM card	cash	medication	plane ticket	swimsuit
backpack	first-aid kit	money belt	sandals	travel insurance
carry-on bag	hiking boots	passport	suitcase	vaccination

Clothing	Money	Health	Documents	Luggage

B **PAIR WORK** What are the five most important items you need for these vacations?

a beach vacation   a rafting trip   a trip to a foreign country

5 INTERCHANGE 5 Fun trips

Decide between two vacations. Student A, go to Interchange 5A
on page 118; Student B, go to Interchange 5B on page 120.

6 PERSPECTIVES Travel advisor

A Listen to these pieces of advice from experienced travelers.
What topic is each person talking about?

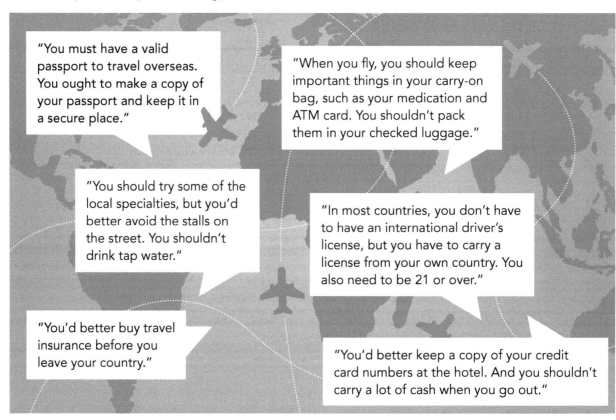

"You must have a valid passport to travel overseas. You ought to make a copy of your passport and keep it in a secure place."

"When you fly, you should keep important things in your carry-on bag, such as your medication and ATM card. You shouldn't pack them in your checked luggage."

"You should try some of the local specialties, but you'd better avoid the stalls on the street. You shouldn't drink tap water."

"In most countries, you don't have to have an international driver's license, but you have to carry a license from your own country. You also need to be 21 or over."

"You'd better buy travel insurance before you leave your country."

"You'd better keep a copy of your credit card numbers at the hotel. And you shouldn't carry a lot of cash when you go out."

B **PAIR WORK** Look at the advice again. Do you think this is all good advice? Why or why not?

7 GRAMMAR FOCUS

▶ **Modals for necessity and suggestion**

Describing necessity	Giving suggestions
You **must** have health insurance.	You**'d better** avoid the stalls on the street.
You **need to** be 21 or over.	You **ought to** make a copy of your passport.
You **have to** get a passport.	You **should** try some local specialties.
You **don't have to** get vaccinations.	You **shouldn't** carry a lot of cash.

GRAMMAR PLUS see page 136

A Choose the best advice for someone who is going on vacation. Then compare with a partner.

1. You _____ pack too many clothes. You won't have room to bring back any gifts. (don't have to / shouldn't)

2. You _____ carry identification with you. It's the law! (must / should)

3. You _____ buy a money belt to carry your passport, ATM card, and cash. (have to / ought to)

4. You _____ make hotel reservations in advance. It might be difficult to find a room after you get there. (have to / 'd better)

5. You _____ buy a round-trip plane ticket because it's cheaper. (must / should)

6. You _____ check out of most hotel rooms by noon if you don't want to pay for another night. (need to / ought to)

B **PAIR WORK** Imagine you're going to travel abroad. Take turns giving each other advice.

"You must take enough medication for your entire trip."

1. You . . . take enough medication for your entire trip.

2. You . . . take your ATM card with you.

3. You . . . get the necessary vaccinations.

4. You . . . forget to pack your camera.

5. You . . . have a visa to enter some foreign countries.

6. You . . . change money before you go. You can do it when you arrive.

8 PRONUNCIATION Linked sounds with /w/ and /y/

▶ Listen and practice. Notice how some words are linked by a /w/ sound, and other words are linked by a /y/ sound.

/w/
You should know about local conditions.

/w/
You ought to do it right away.

/y/
You shouldn't carry a lot of cash.

/y/
You must be at least 21 years old.

9 LISTENING A pleasant trip

▶ **A** Listen to an interview with a spokeswoman from the London Visitor Center. Number the topics she discusses in the correct order from 1 to 4.

    a. ☐ money _____
    b. ☐ public transportation _____
    c. ☐ safety _____
    d. ☐ planning a trip _____

▶ **B** Listen again. Write one piece of advice that she gives for each topic.

    C **GROUP WORK** Which pieces of advice for London apply to your city or town? Which don't? Why and why not?

10 WRITING Have a safe trip.

    A Imagine someone is going to visit your town, city, or country. Write an email giving some suggestions for sightseeing activities.

    ● ● ●   Reply Forward

Dear Michael,

I'm so glad you're coming to visit me in Valparaiso. There are lots of things to see here, and we are going to walk a lot, so bring some comfortable shoes. Don't forget your swimsuit, because I'm planning to take you to Vina del Mar for a day at the beach. It will be warm, so you don't need to pack . . .

Valparaiso, Chile

    B **PAIR WORK** Exchange emails. Is there anything else the visitor needs to know about (food, money, business hours, etc.)?

11 DISCUSSION Around the world

    A **PAIR WORK** You just won a free 30-day trip around the world. Discuss the following questions.

When will you leave and return?
Which direction will you go (east, west, north, or south)?
Where will you choose to stop? Why?
How will you get from place to place?
How long will you stay in each place?

    B **PAIR WORK** What do you need to do before you go? Discuss these topics.

shopping	documents	reservations
packing	money	vaccinations

    A: I think we'd better buy new suitcases.
    B: Good idea. And we should check the weather before we pack.

A Skim the article. Match paragraphs A, B, and C to the photos.

ADVENTURE  VACATIONS

| Home | About | Vacations | Hot spots | Discounts |

A good vacation, for many people, means comfortable accommodations, a great atmosphere, and tasty food. It's a pleasant, relaxing experience. But for some, this type of vacation just isn't enough!

In today's world, many of us have safe, sometimes boring lives. We work, sleep, eat, and watch TV. So more and more people are looking for adventure. They want excitement and danger. They might even want to feel a little afraid!

_____ A How about staying on a desert island in the middle of the Indian Ocean? If you want, you can spend your whole vacation completely alone. You'll sleep in a tent and go fishing for your food. Your only company will be the monkeys and lizards. But don't worry. If you get bored, just call the travel company and they'll send a boat to pick you up!

_____ B Or how about spending a week in the sub-zero temperatures of the North? You will fly to the Arctic, and the local Sami people will teach you to survive in this very difficult environment. You'll learn how to keep yourself warm and make special snowshoes. You can also go ice-fishing and look after reindeer. You'll even learn how to tell when it is going to snow.

_____ C But if the Arctic's too cold, you could try the heat of the jungle instead. Deep in the Amazon rain forest, you'll sleep in the open air. At first, you'll spend a week with local guides. They will train you to do many things, like find food and water or light fires with stones. They will even teach you to pick the tastiest insects for dinner! Then you'll spend a week by yourself with no tent, no extra clothes, and no cell phone. You'll be completely alone – except for the crocodiles and snakes, of course!

B Read the article. Then complete the summary using words from the article.

Nowadays, life can sometimes be a little boring. So, many people are searching for an exciting or dangerous **1)** _____ during their vacations. Some people like the idea of visiting a desert island. There, they spend nights in a **2)** _____ and look for fruit and other plants to eat. If they decide to go to the Arctic instead, they will walk around with unusual **3)** _____ on their feet, and they'll have the experience of taking care of **4)** _____. If they decide to choose a trip to the rain forest, they'll learn many things from **5)** _____, and afterward, they'll live for a whole **6)** _____ completely alone.

C Read the comments of people who are on one of these three trips. Which vacation are they on? Write the letter.

_____ 1. "I know what the weather will be like tomorrow."
_____ 2. "I haven't seen anybody since the moment I arrived."
_____ 3. "My whole body is absolutely freezing!"
_____ 4. "I've learned so much these first seven days."
_____ 5. "I've had enough now! I'm going to call for help."
_____ 6. "I haven't eaten anything like this before!"

D **GROUP WORK** Which of these three vacations would you be prepared to try? Which would you refuse to go on? Why?

6 Sure! I'll do it.

▶ Discuss common complaints
▶ Make and respond to requests
▶ Apologize

1 SNAPSHOT

FAMILY COMPLAINTS

☐ We never have dinner together as a family.
☐ Everybody is always arguing about housework.
☐ My daughter never takes her headphones off.
☐ My father criticizes everything I do.
☐ My husband never helps around the house.
☐ My kids are always texting their friends.
☐ My mother often calls me late at night.
☐ My parents don't respect my privacy.
☐ My brother never puts his phone away.
☐ My wife always brings work home on weekends.

Which complaints seem reasonable? Which ones seem unreasonable? Why?
Do you have similar complaints about anyone in your family? Check (✓) the complaints.
What other complaints do people sometimes have about family members?

2 CONVERSATION I'll turn it off.

▶ **A** Listen and practice.

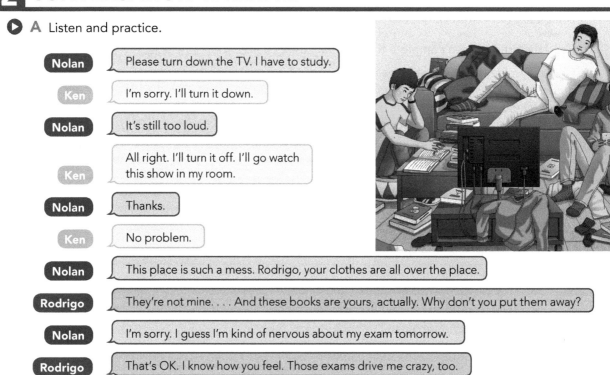

Nolan Please turn down the TV. I have to study.

Ken I'm sorry. I'll turn it down.

Nolan It's still too loud.

Ken All right. I'll turn it off. I'll go watch this show in my room.

Nolan Thanks.

Ken No problem.

Nolan This place is such a mess. Rodrigo, your clothes are all over the place.

Rodrigo They're not mine. . . . And these books are yours, actually. Why don't you put them away?

Nolan I'm sorry. I guess I'm kind of nervous about my exam tomorrow.

Rodrigo That's OK. I know how you feel. Those exams drive me crazy, too.

▶ **B** Listen to the rest of the conversation. What complaints do Nolan and Rodrigo have about Ken?

3 GRAMMAR FOCUS

▶ Two-part verbs; *will* for responding to requests

With nouns	With pronouns	Requests and responses
Turn down the TV.	**Turn** it **down**.	Please turn down the music.
Turn the TV **down**.	(NOT: ~~Turn down it.~~)	OK. I'**ll** turn it down.
Put away your books.	**Put** them **away**.	Put away your books, please.
Put your books **away**.	(NOT: ~~Put away them.~~)	All right. I'**ll** put them away.

GRAMMAR PLUS *see page 137*

A Complete the requests with these words. Then compare with a partner.

your boots	your socks	your jacket	the cat	the trash
the TV	✓ the lights	the magazines	the music	the yard

1. Turn ___the lights___ off, please.
2. Turn _____ on, please.
3. Please turn _____ down.
4. Pick up _____, please.
5. Please put _____ away.

6. Hang _____ up, please.
7. Please take _____ off.
8. Clean _____ up, please.
9. Please take _____ out.
10. Please let _____ out.

B PAIR WORK Take turns making the requests above. Respond with pronouns.

A: Turn the lights off, please.
B: No problem. I'll turn them off.

4 PRONUNCIATION Stress in two-part verbs

▶ **A** Listen and practice. Both words in a two-part verb receive equal stress.

●	●	•	●		●	•	●	●		●	•	●
Pick	up	your	things.		Pick	your	things	up.		Pick	them	up.
Turn	off	the	light.		Turn	the	light	off.		Turn	it	off.

B Write four more requests using the verbs in Exercise 3.
Then practice with a partner. Pay attention to stress.

Sure! I'll do it. **37**

5 WORD POWER Housework

A Find a phrase that is usually paired with each two-part verb. (Some phrases go with more than one verb.) Then add one more phrase for each verb.

the garbage	the magazines	the microwave	your coat
the groceries	the mess	the towels	your laptop

clean up   _____   _____   take out   _____   _____

hang up   _____   _____   throw out   _____   _____

pick up   _____   _____   turn off   _____   _____

put away   _____   _____   turn on   _____   _____

B What requests can you make in each of these rooms? Write four requests and four excuses. Use two-part verbs.

the kitchen   the living room

the bathroom   the bedroom

C **PAIR WORK** Take turns making the requests you wrote in part B. Respond by giving an excuse.

A: Marabel, please pick up the wet towel you left on your bed.

B: Sorry, I can't pick it up right now. I have to put my new clothes away.

6 LISTENING Helping around the house

A Listen to the results of a survey about family life. Check (✓) the answer to each question. Sometimes more than one answer is possible.

	Men	Women	Boys	Girls
1. Who is the messiest in the house?				
2. Who does most of the work in the kitchen?				
3. Who does the general chores inside and outside the house?				
4. Who worries most about expenses?				

B Listen again. According to the survey, what specific chores do men, women, boys, and girls usually do? Take notes.

C **GROUP WORK** How does your family compare to the survey results? Who helps the most with general chores around the house? Who helps the least?

▶ **A** Match the sentences. Then listen and check your answers. Are all the requests reasonable?

1. "Would you take your garbage out, please? ____
2. "Would you mind not parking your car in my parking space? ____
3. "Would you mind turning the music down, please? ____
4. "Could you close the door behind you and make sure it locks? ____
5. "Can you keep your cat inside, please? ____

a. We don't want strangers to enter the building."
b. It often comes into my apartment through the balcony."
c. It can attract insects."
d. The walls are really thin, so the sound goes through to my apartment."
e. I need to park mine there."

B Look at the requests again. Have you ever made similar requests? Has anyone ever asked you to do similar things?

8 GRAMMAR FOCUS

▶ **Requests with modals and *Would you mind . . . ?***

Modal + simple form of verb	**Would you mind . . . + gerund**
Can you **keep** your cat inside, please?	**Would you mind keeping** your cat inside?
Could you **turn** the music **down**, please?	**Would you mind turning** the music **down**, please?
Would you please **park** your car in your space?	**Would you mind not parking** your car in my space?

GRAMMAR PLUS *see page 137*

A Match the requests in column A with the appropriate responses in column B. Then compare with a partner and practice them. (More than one answer may be possible.)

A
1. Would you mind not using your phone in class? ____
2. Would you mind speaking more quietly? ____
3. Would you please turn on the air conditioner? ____
4. Can you make me a sandwich? ____
5. Can you help me with my homework? ____
6. Could you lend me twenty dollars, please? ____

B
a. Sure, no problem. I'd be glad to.
b. Sorry. We didn't know we were so loud.
c. Sure. Do you want anything to drink?
d. Sorry. I had to talk to my boss.
e. I'm sorry, I can't. I don't have any cash.
f. I'm really sorry, but I'm busy.

B **PAIR WORK** Take turns making the requests in part A. Give your own responses.

C **CLASS ACTIVITY** Think of five unusual requests. Go around the class and make your requests. How many people accept? How many refuse?

A: Would you please lend me your car for the weekend?
B: Oh, I'm sorry. I'm going to wash it.

9 SPEAKING Apologies

Choose one of the situations below. Take turns making a request to your "neighbor." The "neighbor" should apologize by giving an excuse, admitting a mistake, or making an offer or a promise.

A: Would you mind not making so much noise? It's very late.
B: Oh, I'm sorry. I didn't realize it bothered you.

Different ways to apologize

give an excuse	"I'm sorry. I didn't realize . . ."
admit a mistake	"I forgot I left it there."
make an offer	"I'll take it out right now."
make a promise	"I promise I'll . . ./I'll make sure to . . ."

10 INTERCHANGE 6 I'm terribly sorry.

How good are you at apologizing? Go to Interchange 6 on page 119.

11 WRITING A public message

A Think of a problem that you could have with your neighbors.
Write a message explaining the problem and making a request.

> To the person who left a big mess in the laundry room yesterday afternoon:
> Would you mind cleaning up after you finish your laundry? I fell down and
> almost broke my leg because the floor was all wet. Thank you.

B **PAIR WORK** Exchange messages with your classmates.
Write a message apologizing for the problem you caused
to your "neighbor."

> I'm sorry about the mess in the laundry room. My boss called me, and
> I had to go back to the office. I'll make sure to clean it up next time.

C **GROUP WORK** Take turns reading your messages aloud. Do you have similar
problems with your neighbors? How do you solve them?

A Scan the text. How many of the requests and complaints are about food?

HOME   WORLD   CULTURE   TRAVEL   BUSINESS   SPORTS   FOOD

HOTEL MADNESS: THE CRAZY THINGS PEOPLE SAY!

There are about 500,000 hotels around the world. Every day, receptionists, servers, chefs, and managers work in these hotels looking after their guests. Guests often make special requests for things like an extra-large bed or a room with a view of the water. And sometimes people complain when something is not satisfactory. In the U.S., around two-thirds of these complaints are about the noise that other guests are making. Sometimes, guests' requests and complaints can make a hotel worker's job almost impossible!

Here are some very weird requests that hotel workers have actually heard:

"Would you mind lending me your suit tomorrow? I have a job interview to go to!"

"Could one of the staff give my daughter a hand with her homework?"

"Can you please fill my bath with chocolate milk?"

"I'd like chicken for dinner, please, but only the right leg."

"Can you make sure all the strawberries in my cereal are the same size?"

Some hotel guests are also very good at finding (or imagining) problems! These are some of their crazy complaints:

At a London hotel, 40 miles from the coast: "I can't see the ocean from my room."

I think I'd look good in that jacket.

Well, sir, we always try to help, but . . .

At a Portuguese hotel: "My bed is way too comfortable. I keep oversleeping and missing the best part of the day!"

At a hotel in Spain: "There are too many tasty dishes on the restaurant buffet. I've gained more than 5 pounds!"

To a receptionist in the middle of the night: "I haven't been able to sleep at all! My wife won't stop snoring!"

After coming back from a day trip to a water park: "Nobody told us to bring our swimsuits and towels."

So the next time you're at a hotel and the staff look tired, be patient! Maybe they've had a stressful day!

B Read the article. Find the words in *italics* in the article. Then match each word with its meaning.

1. *give (somebody) a hand* ____
2. *satisfactory* ____
3. *weird* ____
4. *snoring* ____
5. *oversleep* ____

a. to breathe in a noisy way when asleep
b. help a person do something
c. good enough
d. not wake up early enough
e. very strange

C The sentences below are false. Correct each sentence to make it true.

1. It's common for guests to request a bigger room.
2. One hotel guest asked to borrow an employee's dress.
3. Another guest wanted the fruit at breakfast to be the same color.
4. One person wasn't happy because he kept getting up too early.
5. Someone complained about not taking the right things to go sightseeing.

D PAIR WORK Imagine you are the managers of a hotel. How would you respond to the requests and complaints above? Try to be as polite as you can!

Units 5–6 Progress check

How well can you do these things? Check (✓) the boxes.

I can . . .	Very well	OK	A little
Understand descriptions of people's plans (Ex. 1)	☐	☐	☐
Discuss vacation plans (Ex. 2)	☐	☐	☐
Give travel advice (Ex. 2)	☐	☐	☐
Make and respond to requests (Ex. 3, 4)	☐	☐	☐
Apologize and give excuses (Ex. 3, 4)	☐	☐	☐

1 LISTENING What are your plans?

▶ **A** Listen to Lily, Tyler, and Abby describe their summer plans. What is each person going to do?

Summer plans	Reason
1. Lily	
2. Tyler	
3. Abby	

▶ **B** Listen again. What is the reason for each person's choice?

C **PAIR WORK** What did you do last summer? Listen to your partner and share with the class.

2 DISCUSSION Vacation plans

A **GROUP WORK** Imagine you are going to go on vacation. Take turns asking and answering these questions.

A: Where are you going to go on your next vacation?
B: I'm going to go to New York.
A: What are you going to do?
B: I'm going to visit the museums. Maybe I'll see a musical on Broadway.
A: Why did you choose that?
B: Well, I want to have a more cultural vacation this year.

B **GROUP WORK** What should each person do to prepare for his or her vacation? Give each other advice.

3 ROLE PLAY Making excuses

Student A: Your partner was supposed to do some things, but didn't. Look at the pictures and make a request about each one.

Student B: You were supposed to do some things, but didn't. Listen to your partner's requests. Apologize and either agree to the request or give an excuse.

A: Your room is a big mess. Please clean it up.

B: I'm sorry. I forgot about it. I'll clean it up after dinner.

Change roles and try the role play again.

4 GAME Can I ask you a favor?

A Write three requests on separate cards. Put an X on the back of two of the cards.

> Can you help me with my homework?

> Could you get me a cup of coffee?

> Would you mind cooking dinner tonight?

B CLASS ACTIVITY Shuffle all the cards together. Take three new cards.

Go around the class and take turns making requests with the cards. Hold up each card so your classmate can see the back.

When answering:

X on the back = refuse the request and give an excuse

No X = agree to the request

Can you help me with my homework?

I'm sorry, I can't. I'm . . .

WHAT'S NEXT?

Look at your Self-assessment again. Do you need to review anything?

7 What do you use this for?

▸ Describe uses and purposes of technology
▸ Give suggestions

1 SNAPSHOT

Inventions We Can't Live Without

☐ smartphones
☐ digital cameras
☐ Internet
☐ e-readers
☐ tablet computers
☐ streaming TV

☐ robots
☐ 3-D printers
☐ driverless cars
☐ GPS technology
☐ drones
☐ Wi-Fi

How long have the inventions above been around in your country?
How was life different before them?
Check (✓) three inventions you couldn't live without. Compare with a partner.

2 PERSPECTIVES Smartphone usage

▶ **A** How do you use your smartphone? Listen and respond to the statements.

I use my smartphone . . .	Often	Sometimes	Hardly ever	Never
to send messages	☐	☐	☐	☐
for watching videos	☐	☐	☐	☐
to take photos	☐	☐	☐	☐
to post on social media sites	☐	☐	☐	☐
for doing school assignments	☐	☐	☐	☐
to send emails	☐	☐	☐	☐
to shop online	☐	☐	☐	☐
to check the weather	☐	☐	☐	☐
to read e-books	☐	☐	☐	☐
for listening to music	☐	☐	☐	☐

B **PAIR WORK** Compare your answers. Are your answers similar or different?

3 GRAMMAR FOCUS

▶ **Infinitives and gerunds for uses and purposes**

Infinitives	Gerunds
I use my cell phone **to send** messages.	I use my cell phone **for sending** messages.
Some people use their phones **to watch** videos.	Some people use their phones **for watching** videos.
People often use their phones **to take** photos.	People often use their phones **for taking** photos.

GRAMMAR PLUS *see page 138*

A PAIR WORK What do you know about this technology? Complete the sentences in column A with information from column B. Use infinitives and gerunds. (More than one combination is possible.)

A	B
1. Many people use tablet computers . . .	look for criminals.
2. You can use your smartphone . . .	perform dangerous tasks.
3. Engineers use 3-D printers . . .	get directions.
4. People can use the Internet . . .	make car parts.
5. Companies sometimes use robots . . .	make video calls.
6. The police use drones . . .	learn languages.

> Many people use tablet computers to make video calls.
> Many people use tablet computers for making video calls.

B PAIR WORK Think of one other use for the items in column A.

"Paparazzi use drones to spy on celebrities."

C GROUP WORK List some unexpected uses for these new and old items. Compare your answers with the whole class. Who came up with the most uses?

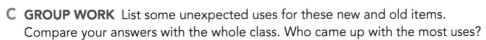

| a smartphone | a paper clip | a webcam | a pencil | invisible tape | an old CD |

"You can use your smartphone for driving your car."

4 PRONUNCIATION Syllable stress

▶ **A** Listen and practice. Notice which syllable has the main stress.

● ● ●	● ● ●	● ● ●
Internet	invention	engineer
messages	assignment	DVD
digital	computer	recommend
_____	_____	_____
_____	_____	_____

▶ **B** Where is the stress in these words? Add them to the columns in part A. Then listen and check.

directions   driverless   entertain   equipment   media   understand

5 WORD POWER Plugged in

A Complete the chart with words and phrases from the list. Add one more to each category. Then compare with a partner.

✓ computer whiz	hacker	check in for a flight	geek
computer crash	edit photos	download apps	software bugs
flash drive	identity theft	make international phone calls	frozen screen
smart devices	early adopter	solar-powered batteries	phone charger

Problems with technology	Gadgets and devices	People who are "into" technology	Things to do online
		computer whiz	

B **GROUP WORK** Discuss some of the positive and negative consequences of living in a connected world.

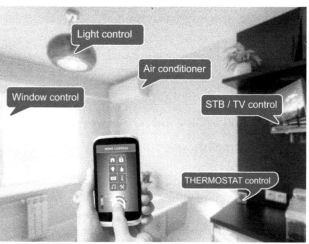

- Have you ever had any of the problems mentioned in part A? What happened? What did you do?
- Do you have any smart devices? Which ones? How do they help you? How much do you depend on them?
- Do you have any friends who never put their phone away? Is anyone in your family addicted to new technologies? Are you?
- What is one gadget you would really like to have? Why?
- Is identity theft a problem where you live? What about hackers? How do you protect against them?

6 LISTENING They've thought of everything!

▶ A Listen to two people talk about the best apps for travel. Check (✓) the four app categories. (There are two extra categories.)

- ☐ safety _____
- ☐ packing _____
- ☐ music _____
- ☐ transportation _____
- ☐ attractions _____
- ☐ hotel _____

▶ B Listen again. What can you use the apps for? Write the uses next to the categories you checked above.

C **PAIR WORK** What are your favorite apps? Discuss and share with the class.

7 CONVERSATION What do I do now?

▶ **A** Listen and practice.

Justin: I can't believe my phone's frozen again.

Allie: How long have you had it?

Justin: About a year. It's not that old.

Allie: Maybe someone hacked it.

Justin: Really? You think so?

Allie: No, I'm just kidding. It's probably just a virus.

Justin: Oh. So what do I do now?

Allie: First, you'd better install a good antivirus app. And be sure to update it.

Justin: OK, I'll download one now. What else should I do?

Allie: Well, don't forget to reset all your passwords.

Justin: That's a good idea. I never remember to change my passwords.

Allie: One more thing. Try not to use public Wi-Fi networks.

Justin: You're right. I have to learn to be more careful.

▶ **B** Listen to the rest of the conversation. What else does Justin want help with? What does Allie suggest?

8 GRAMMAR FOCUS

▶
Imperatives and infinitives for giving suggestions

Be sure to update the app.

Make sure to charge your phone.

Remember to back up your files.

Don't forget to reset your passwords.

Try not to use public Wi-Fi networks.

GRAMMAR PLUS *see page 138*

A Look at the suggestions. Rewrite them using these phrases. Then compare with a partner.

Make sure to . . .   Try to . . .   Remember to . . .

Be sure not to . . .   Try not to . . .   Don't forget to . . .

1. **a.** Before using an electronic safe, you have to reset the passcode.
   b. You should check if it's locked after you close it.
2. **a.** Don't get your phone wet or it might not work anymore.
   b. It's important to back up your contacts and other important information.
3. **a.** You must set your alarm system each time you leave home.
   b. Don't use your birthday as a code.
4. **a.** You ought to keep the lenses of your digital camera clean.
   b. It's important to keep the lens cap on when you're not taking photos.

B **PAIR WORK** Take turns giving other suggestions for using the items in part A.

9 LISTENING Smart suggestions

▶ A Listen to people give suggestions for using three of these things.
Number them 1, 2, and 3. (There are two extra things.)

☐

portable speaker

☐

GPS system

☐

flash drive

☐

smartphone

☐

ATM card

▶ B Listen again. Write two suggestions you hear for each thing. Then compare with a partner.

1. _____   _____

2. _____   _____

3. _____   _____

C PAIR WORK What do you know about the other two things in part A? Give suggestions about them.
"Be sure to buy one with lots of memory."

10 INTERCHANGE 7 Free advice

Give your classmates some advice. Go to Interchange 7 on page 121.

11 WRITING A message

A Imagine your brother is coming over for dinner, but you are going to be busy all day. Your roommate has agreed to help you. Think of three things you need help with. Then write a message with instructions.

B GROUP WORK Take turns reading your messages aloud. Did you ask for similar favors?

60%

CALLS   CHATS   CONTACTS

Hi, Melissa. Thanks a lot for your help. Please remember to do these three things. First, make sure to buy some groceries. The shopping list is on the refrigerator. Also, please don't forget to . . .

A Skim the article. What is the sharing economy? What three examples does the article give?

THE SHARING ECONOMY – GOOD FOR EVERYBODY?

Modern technology has made it easier for ordinary people to rent things or services to others. With the click of an app, we can find almost anything. It could be a new dress to wear on the weekend, or someone to clean your house. This is the sharing economy, and it is now a profitable $20 billion-a-year business. But some people are now asking: Just how good is it for society in general?

Not long ago, when people went on vacation, they usually stayed in a hotel. Today they have the choice of staying in someone's private house. They pay less, but what effect does this have on the hotel industry and the wider economy? Hotels receive fewer guests, but they still have to pay salaries to their employees and taxes to the government. Many people who rent out rooms do not. So the government gets less money, and some hotels might even close down.

Then there are car-sharing sites. Instead of using your own car for a long trip you can get a ride with someone for a small fee. Some people argue this is better for the environment, since fewer cars on the roads means less pollution. But how many people choose to use these sites rather than taking the bus or the train? Public transportation is, after all, much kinder to the environment than cars.

Many sites offer cooking services. Instead of going to a restaurant, you can use an app to order dishes from people in your neighborhood.

There is even a site where you can buy leftover food that people haven't eaten! This is sure to save you time and money. But is it risky? Can you trust the people cooking your food? Restaurants have to follow strict regulations to make sure their food is safe to eat.

There is no doubt that the sharing economy is growing. Some economists think it will be worth $335 billion by 2025. As new technology makes sharing food, accommodation, and transportation easier all the time, the question of "Is it fair?" will remain.

B Read the article. Find the words in *italics* below. Then circle the meaning of each word.

1. When a business is *profitable*, it **makes / loses** money.
2. *Taxes* are money that people **give to / receive from** the government.
3. If something is *risky*, it's **dangerous / safe**.
4. *Regulations* are **rules / people** that control how we do things.
5. When something is *fair*, everybody has **equal / different** opportunities.

C Answer the questions.

1. How much is the sharing economy worth nowadays?
2. What is the advantage of staying in a private house instead of a hotel?
3. Why is car sharing less damaging to the environment?
4. What is better for the environment than car sharing?
5. How can buying food from non-professionals be risky?

D Do you use any of these sharing-economy services? Are they ever risky? Do you think they are fair?

Time to celebrate!

▸ Discuss holidays and special occasions
▸ Describe celebrations, annual events, and customs

1 SNAPSHOT

HOLIDAYS AND FESTIVALS

Day of the Dead
November 2nd

Mexicans make playful skeleton sculptures and bake *pan de muerto* – bread of the dead.

Thanksgiving
November

In the United States, families get together, have a traditional meal, and give thanks for life and health.

Saint Patrick's Day
March 17th

People of Irish background wear green to celebrate their culture with parades, dancing, parties, and special foods.

Chinese New Year
January or February

Chinese people celebrate the lunar new year with fireworks and dragon dances.

Do you celebrate these or similar holidays in your country?
What other special days do you have?
What's your favorite holiday or festival?

2 WORD POWER Ways to celebrate

A Which word or phrase is not usually paired with each verb?
Put a line through it. Then compare with a partner.

1. **eat**	candy	sweets	~~a mask~~
2. **give**	presents	a celebration	money
3. **go to**	decorations	a wedding	a party
4. **have a**	picnic	beach	meal
5. **play**	games	candles	music
6. **send**	cards	flowers	a barbecue
7. **visit**	relatives	food	close friends
8. **watch**	a birthday	a parade	fireworks
9. **wear**	costumes	invitations	traditional clothes

B **PAIR WORK** Do you do any of the things in part A as part of a cultural or family celebration? When? Tell your partner.

3 PERSPECTIVES Favorite celebrations

▶ **A** Listen to these comments about special days of the year. Match them to the correct pictures.

____ **1.** "My favorite celebration is Mother's Day. It's a day when my husband and my kids make pancakes for me – just like I used to make for my mom – and I get to have breakfast in bed."

____ **2.** "February 14th is the day when people give cards and presents to the ones they love. I'm really looking forward to Valentine's Day! I already have a gift for my boyfriend."

____ **3.** "New Year's Eve is a night when I have fun with my friends. We usually have a big party. We stay up all night and then go out for breakfast in the morning."

B **PAIR WORK** What do you like about each celebration in part A?

4 GRAMMAR FOCUS

▶ **Relative clauses of time**

Mother's Day is **a day**	**when** my kids make pancakes for me.
February 14th is **the day**	**when** people give cards to the ones they love.
New Year's Eve is **a night**	**when** I have fun with my friends.

GRAMMAR PLUS *see page 139*

A How much do you know about these times? Complete the sentences in column A with information from column B. Then compare with a partner.

A
1. Mother's Day is a day when _____
2. New Year's Eve is a night when _____
3. April Fools' Day is a day when _____
4. Valentine's Day is a day when _____
5. Labor Day is a day when _____
6. Summer is a time when _____

B
a. people sometimes play tricks on friends.
b. people celebrate their mothers.
c. many people like to go to the beach.
d. people in many countries honor workers.
e. people express their love to someone.
f. people have parties with family and friends.

B Complete these sentences with your own information. Then compare with a partner.

Winter is the season . . .   Children's Day is a day . . .

Birthdays are days . . .   July and August are the months . . .

Spring is the time of year . . .   A wedding anniversary is a time . . .

5 LISTENING Time for Carnival!

Carnival in Brazil

▶ **A** Listen to Vanessa talk about her trip to Carnival in Brazil. Write three facts about Carnival that she mentions.

▶ **B** Listen again and answer these questions about Vanessa's experience.

Why did she have to book her hotel six months early?
What happened when Vanessa got lost?
What was her favorite thing about Carnival? Why?

C **PAIR WORK** Think of another famous celebration that is similar to Carnival. Describe it to the class. They will try to guess the celebration.

6 SPEAKING Favorite holidays

A **PAIR WORK** Choose your three favorite holidays. Tell your partner why you like each one.

A: I really like Independence Day.
B: What do you like about it?
A: It's a day when we watch parades and fireworks.
B: Do you do anything special?
A: We usually have a barbecue. My father makes burgers, and my mother makes her special potato salad.

B **CLASS ACTIVITY** Take a class vote. What are the most popular holidays in your class?

7 WRITING An online entry

A Write an entry for a travel website about a festival or celebration where you live. When is it? How do people celebrate it? What should a visitor see and do?

Obon is an annual event when Japanese people commemorate their ancestors. They visit and clean the graves of their dead relatives. People put candles in lanterns and float them on rivers. There are neighborhood dances at parks, gardens, and . . .

read more

B **PAIR WORK** Read your partner's entry. What do you like about it? Can you suggest anything to improve it?

8 CONVERSATION A traditional wedding

▶ **A** Listen and practice.

JULIA Is this a picture from your wedding, Anusha?

ANUSHA Yes. We had the ceremony in India.

JULIA And was this your wedding dress?

ANUSHA Yes. It's a sari, actually. In India, when women get married, they usually wear a brightly colored sari, not a white dress.

JULIA It's beautiful! So, what are weddings like in India?

ANUSHA Well, in some traditions, after the groom arrives, the bride and groom exchange garlands of flowers. We did that. But we didn't do some other traditional things.

JULIA Oh? Like what?

ANUSHA Well, before the wedding, the bride's female relatives usually have a party to celebrate. But I'm an only child, and I don't have any female cousins, so we skipped that.

JULIA That makes sense. You know, I have heard about this one tradition . . . When the groom takes off his shoes, the bride's sisters steal them! I guess you didn't do that, either?

ANUSHA Oh, no, we did that part. My mom stole them!

▶ **B** Listen to the rest of the conversation.
What does Anusha say about her wedding reception?

9 PRONUNCIATION Stress and rhythm

▶ **A** Listen and practice. Notice how stressed words and syllables occur with a regular rhythm.

●   ●   ●   ●   ●   ●   ●

When women get married, they usually wear a brightly colored sari.

▶ **B** Listen to the stress and rhythm in these sentences. Then practice them.
1. After the groom arrives, the bride and groom exchange garlands of flowers.
2. Before the wedding, the bride's female relatives usually have a party to celebrate.
3. When the groom takes off his shoes, the bride's sisters steal them.

10 GRAMMAR FOCUS

▶ **Adverbial clauses of time**

When women get married,	they usually wear a brightly colored sari.
After the groom arrives,	the bride and groom exchange garlands of flowers.
Before the wedding,	the bride's female relatives usually have a party to celebrate.

GRAMMAR PLUS *see page 139*

A What do you know about wedding customs in North America?
Complete these sentences with the information below.

1. Before a man and woman get married, they usually ____
2. When a couple gets engaged, the man often ____
3. Right after a couple gets engaged, they usually ____
4. When a woman gets married, she usually ____
5. When guests go to a wedding, they almost always ____
6. Right after a couple gets married, they usually ____

a. wears a long white dress and a veil.
b. go on a short trip called a "honeymoon."
c. give the bride and groom gifts or some money.
d. gives the woman an engagement ring.
e. begin to plan the wedding.
f. date each other for a year or more.

B **PAIR WORK** What happens when people get married in your country?
Tell your partner by completing the statements in part A with your own
information. Pay attention to stress and rhythm.

11 INTERCHANGE 8 It's worth celebrating.

How do your classmates celebrate special occasions? Go to Interchange 8 on page 122.

12 SPEAKING My personal traditions

A **GROUP WORK** How do you usually celebrate the dates below? Share your personal traditions with
your classmates.

your birthday   New Year's Eve   your country's national day   your favorite holiday

A: On my birthday, I always wear new
clothes, and I often have a party.
What about you?
B: I usually celebrate my birthday with my
family. We have a special meal and
some relatives come over.
C: I used to celebrate my birthday at home,
but now I usually go out with friends.

B **CLASS ACTIVITY** Tell the class the most
interesting traditions you talked about in
your group. Do you share any common
traditions? Did you use to celebrate those
dates the same way when you were younger?

A Skim the article. Which of these phrases could be a title for this article?

The best New Year's resolutions New Year's traditions around the world
How to host a New Year's Eve party

Out with the Old, In with THE NEW

It's midnight on New Year's Eve. Clocks are striking twelve as people welcome in the coming year and say goodbye to the old. It's a time when people wish for good luck in the future and forget bad things in the past. Around the world, people do different things to help their wishes come true. Some of <u>them</u> might surprise you.

Food is often central to New Year's customs. In Ireland, they hit the walls and doors of their houses with loaves of bread. They hope <u>this</u> will make good luck enter the house and bad luck leave it. The Spanish and the Mexicans eat twelve grapes in twelve seconds – <u>one</u> for luck in each of the coming months. Eating grapes so fast isn't easy, but it's fun and often messy!

Colors are important, too. Brazilians, for example, choose their clothes very carefully – for peace they wear white, yellow might bring success, and red means love is in the air! The Chinese believe red brings good luck, so they like to dress in this color, too. They also give family members and friends red envelopes containing money.

Some people destroy things on New Year's Eve because they want to forget the past. In Ecuador and Colombia, people make a dummy and fill it with sawdust, newspaper, or old clothes. <u>They</u> dress it, put a mask on it, and name it after someone famous or a friend or family member. Then they burn it.

And some customs have no reason at all; <u>they</u> just develop over time. On New Year's Eve in Germany, several TV stations show a short black-and-white movie called *Dinner for One*. It's a comedy in English, starring English actors. Nobody knows why they do this, not even the Germans!

B Read the article. Check (✓) True or False for each statement about New Year's customs. Then correct each false statement.

	True	False	
1. In Ireland, people eat loaves of bread for good luck.	☐	☐	
2. They eat apples for good luck in Spain.	☐	☐	
3. In China, people change the color of their doors.	☐	☐	
4. In Colombia, they burn a doll with old things inside.	☐	☐	
5. In Germany, people watch *Dinner for One* because it's about New Year's Eve.	☐	☐	

C What do the underlined words in the article refer to? Write the correct word.

1. them _____ **3.** one _____ **5.** they _____
2. this _____ **4.** They _____

D What do people in your country do for the New Year? What is your favorite New Year's tradition?

SELF-ASSESSMENT

How well can you do these things? Check (✓) the boxes.

I can . . .	Very well	OK	A little
Describe uses and purposes of objects (Ex. 1)	☐	☐	☐
Give instructions and suggestions (Ex. 2)	☐	☐	☐
Describe holidays and special occasions (Ex. 3, 5)	☐	☐	☐
Understand descriptions of customs (Ex. 4, 5)	☐	☐	☐
Ask and answer questions about celebrations and customs (Ex. 5)	☐	☐	☐

1 GAME Guess my object.

A **PAIR WORK** Think of five familiar objects. Write a short description of each object's use and purpose. Don't write the name of the objects.

> It's electronic. It's small. It connects to the Internet.
> You wear it. It communicates with your phone.

B **GROUP WORK** Take turns reading your descriptions and guessing the objects. Keep score. Who guessed the most items correctly? Who wrote the best descriptions?

2 ROLE PLAY It's all under control.

Student A: Choose one situation below. Decide on the details and answer Student B's questions. Then get some suggestions.

Start like this: *I'm really nervous. I'm . . .*

giving a speech	**going on a job interview**	**taking my driving test**
What is it about?	What's the job?	When is it?
Where is it?	What are the responsibilities?	How long is it?
How many people will be there?	Who is interviewing you?	Have you prepared?

Student B: Student A is telling you about a situation. Ask the appropriate questions above. Then give some suggestions.

Change roles and try the role play again.

useful expressions	
Try to . . .	Try not to . . .
Remember to . . .	Be sure to . . .
Don't forget to . . .	Make sure to . . .

3 | SPEAKING Unofficial holidays

A **PAIR WORK** Choose one of these holidays or create your own.
Then write a description of the holiday. Answer the questions below.

Buy Nothing Day

National Day of Unplugging

World Smile Day

What is the name of the holiday? When is it?
How do you celebrate it?

B **GROUP WORK** Read your description to the
group. Then vote on the best holiday.

> Buy Nothing Day is a day when you can't buy
> anything. It's a day to think about what we consume,
> what we really need, and how much money we waste.

4 | LISTENING Marriage customs around the world

▶ **A** Listen to two people discuss a book about marriage customs.
Match each country to the title that describes its marriage custom.

1. Sweden ___
2. China ___
3. Paraguay ___
4. Germany ___

a. *Fighting for Love*
b. *Dishes for Good Luck*
c. *Kisses for Guests*
d. *Tears of Happiness*

▶ **B** Listen again. Complete the sentences to describe the custom.

1. When the groom leaves the table, _____.
2. One month before the wedding, _____.
3. When they want to marry the same man, _____.
4. After the guests bring the dishes to the couple, _____.

C **PAIR WORK** Think of some marriage customs from your country.
How are they similar to these customs? How are they different?

5 | DISCUSSION Just married

GROUP WORK Talk about marriage in your country.
Ask these questions and others of your own.

How old are people when they get married?
What happens after a couple gets engaged?
What happens during the ceremony?
What do the bride and groom wear?
What kinds of food is served at the reception?
What kinds of gifts do people usually give?

WHAT'S NEXT?

Look at your Self-assessment again. Do you need to review anything?

Interchange activities

We have a lot in common.

A **CLASS ACTIVITY** Go around the class and find out the information below. Then ask follow-up questions and take notes. Write a classmate's name only once.

Find someone who . . .	Name	Notes
1. wanted to be a movie star **"Did you ever want to be a movie star?"**		
2. always listened to his or her teachers **"Did you always listen to your teachers?"**		
3. used to look very different **"Did you use to look very different?"**		
4. had a pet when he or she was little **"Did you have a pet when you were little?"**		
5. changed schools when he or she was a child "_____?"		
6. used to argue with his or her brothers and sisters "_____?"		
7. got in trouble a lot as a child "_____?"		
8. used to have a favorite toy "_____?"		

B **GROUP WORK** Tell the group the most interesting thing you learned about your classmates.

A **PAIR WORK** Look at the photos and slogans below. What do you think the theme of each tourism campaign is?

Possible themes		
art	culture	entertainment
food	history	music
nature	shopping	sports

Cartagena
"The Colorful Caribbean"

New Orleans
"The Birthplace of Jazz"

Cairo
"The Earth's Mother"

Bangkok
"Thailand Old and New"

B **GROUP WORK** Imagine you are planning a campaign to attract more tourists to one of the cities above or to a city of your choice.
Use the ideas below or your own ideas to discuss the campaign.

a good time to visit
famous historical attractions
special events or festivals
nice areas to stay
interesting places to see
memorable things to do

A: Do you know when a good time to visit Cartagena is?
B: I think between December and April is a good time because . . .

C **GROUP WORK** What will be the theme of your campaign? What slogan will you use?

INTERCHANGE 3 A dream come true

A Complete this questionnaire with information about yourself.

My Wish List

1. What possession do you wish you had?
   I wish I had _____

2. What sport do you wish you could play?
   _____

3. Where do you wish you could live?
   _____

4. What skill do you wish you had?
   _____

5. What kind of home do you wish you could have?
   _____

6. What kind of vacation do you wish you could take?
   _____

7. What languages do you wish you could speak?
   _____

8. Which musical instruments do you wish you could play?
   _____

9. What famous person do you wish you could meet?
   _____

10. What kind of pet do you wish you could have?
    _____

B **PAIR WORK** Compare your questionnaires. Take turns asking and answering questions about your wishes.

A: What possession do you wish you had?
B: I wish I had a sailboat.
A: Really? Why?
B: Well, I could sail around the world!

C **CLASS ACTIVITY** Imagine you are at a class reunion. It is ten years since you completed the questionnaire in part A. Tell the class about some wishes that have come true for your partner.

"Victor is now a famous explorer and sailor. He has sailed across the Atlantic and to the South Pole. Right now, he's writing a book about his adventures on his boat."

A How much do you really know about your classmates? Look at the survey and add two more situations to items 1 and 2.

	Name	Notes
1. Find someone who has . . . 　a. cooked for more than twenty people 　b. found something valuable 　c. lost his or her phone 　d. been on TV 　e. cried during a movie 　f. _____ 　g. _____		
2. Find someone who has never . . . 　a. been camping 　b. gone horseback riding 　c. fallen asleep at the movies 　d. played a video game 　e. baked cookies 　f. _____ 　g. _____		

B CLASS ACTIVITY Go around the class and ask the questions. Write the names of classmates who answer "yes" for item 1 and "no" for item 2. Then ask follow-up questions and take notes.

A: Have you ever cooked for more than 20 people?

B: Yes, I have. Last year I cooked for the whole family on Mother's Day.

A: How was it?

B: Well, my mother had to help me.

A: Have you ever been camping?

C: No, I haven't.

A: Why not?

C: Because I don't like mosquitoes.

C GROUP WORK
Compare the information in your surveys.

STUDENT A

A PAIR WORK You and your partner are going to take a trip. You have a brochure for a surfing trip to Hawaii, and your partner has a brochure for a hiking trip to the Grand Canyon.

First, find out about the hiking trip. Ask your partner questions about these things.

The length of the trip	The cost of the trip	What the price includes
The accommodations	Additional activities	Nighttime activities

B PAIR WORK Now use the information in this brochure to answer your partner's questions about the surfing trip.

SURFING VACATION IN HAWAII

Seven-day surf camp on the magical island of Oahu for surfers of all ability levels

Visit the best attractions on the island:
Kailua Beach Park
The Waikiki Aquarium
Pearl Harbor

Accommodations:
Beachfront studios and apartments

Price includes:
Daily surf lessons
All necessary equipment
Breakfast and lunch

Additional activities:
Catamaran sailing lessons
Snorkeling at Hanauma Bay Beach

Nighttime activities:
Authentic Hawaiian luau
Hula shows

Vacation cost:
$2,100

C PAIR WORK Decide which trip you are going to take. Then explain your choice to the class.

INTERCHANGE 6 I'm terribly sorry.

A PAIR WORK Look at these situations. Act out conversations. Apologize and then give an excuse, admit a mistake, or make an offer or a promise.

useful expressions
I'm sorry. / I didn't realize. / I forgot.   You're right. / I was wrong.
I'll . . . right away.   I'll make sure to . . . / I promise I'll . . .

Student A: You are trying to watch the movie.
Student B: You are talking on your phone.
A: Excuse me. I'm trying to watch the movie. Could you please turn off your phone?
B: I'm so sorry . . .

Student A: You are the server.
Student B: You are one of the customers.
A: Oh, I'm terribly sorry . . .
B: _____

Student A: You have just arrived for the meeting.
Student B: You are making a presentation.
A: I'm sorry I'm late . . .
B: _____

Student A: You are the host.
Student B: You broke the vase.
A: Oh, no! My vase.
B: _____

B GROUP WORK Have you ever experienced situations like these? What happened? What did you do? Share your stories.

Student B

A PAIR WORK You and your partner are going to take a trip. You have a brochure for a hiking trip to the Grand Canyon, and your partner has a brochure for a surfing trip to Hawaii.

First, use the information in the brochure to answer your partner's questions about the hiking trip.

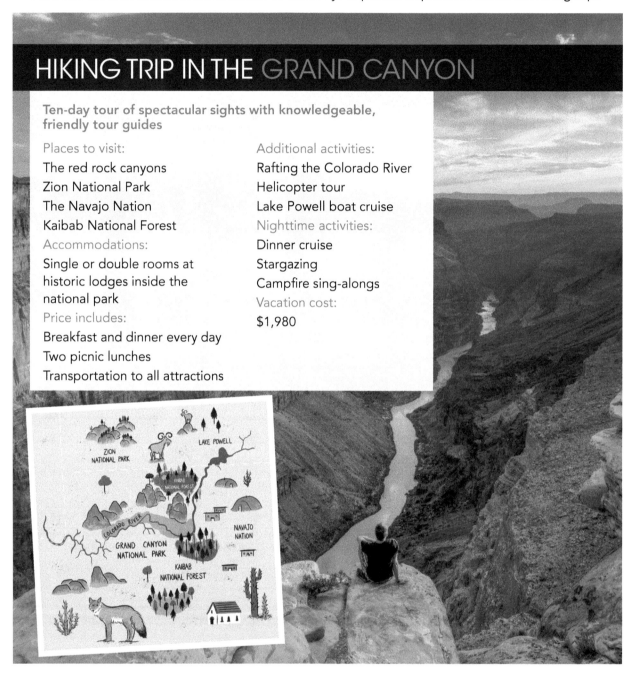

HIKING TRIP IN THE GRAND CANYON

Ten-day tour of spectacular sights with knowledgeable, friendly tour guides

Places to visit:
The red rock canyons
Zion National Park
The Navajo Nation
Kaibab National Forest

Accommodations:
Single or double rooms at historic lodges inside the national park

Price includes:
Breakfast and dinner every day
Two picnic lunches
Transportation to all attractions

Additional activities:
Rafting the Colorado River
Helicopter tour
Lake Powell boat cruise

Nighttime activities:
Dinner cruise
Stargazing
Campfire sing-alongs

Vacation cost:
$1,980

B PAIR WORK Now find out about the surfing trip. Ask your partner questions about these things.

The length of the trip	The cost of the trip	What the price includes
The accommodations	Additional activities	Nighttime activities

C PAIR WORK Decide which trip you are going to take. Then explain your choice to the class.

A **GROUP WORK** Look at the problems people have. What advice would you give each person? Discuss possible suggestions and then choose the best one.

"I'm moving to a new apartment with two roommates. How can I be sure we get along well and avoid problems?"

"A co-worker has asked to borrow my brand-new mountain bike for the weekend. I don't want to lend it. What can I say?"

"My family and I are going away on vacation for two weeks. How can we make sure our home is safe from burglars while we're gone?"

"I have an important job interview next week. How can I make sure to be successful and get the job?"

"I'm going to meet my future in-laws tomorrow for the first time. How can I make a good impression?"

"I'm really into social networking, but in the past week, five people I hardly know have asked to be my friends. What should I do?"

B **PAIR WORK** Choose one of the situations above. Ask your partner for advice. Then give him or her advice about his or her problem.

A: I'm moving to a new apartment with two roommates. How can I be sure we get along well?

B: Make sure you decide how you are going to split the household chores. And remember to . . .

A CLASS ACTIVITY How do your classmates celebrate special occasions? Go around the class and ask the questions below. If someone answers "yes," write down his or her name. Ask for more information and take notes.

Question	Name	Notes
1. Have you ever given someone a surprise party?		
2. What's the best gift you have ever received?		
3. Do you ever wear traditional clothes?		
4. Have you bought flowers for someone special recently?		
5. Do you like to watch parades?		
6. Does your family have big get-togethers?		
7. Has someone given you money recently as a gift?		
8. Will you celebrate your next birthday with a party?		
9. Do you ever give friends birthday presents?		
10. What's your favorite time of the year?		
11. Do you ever celebrate a holiday with fireworks?		

A: Have you ever given someone a surprise party?
B: Yes. Once we gave my co-worker a surprise party on his birthday.
A: How was it?
B: It was great. He never suspected that we were planning it, so he was really surprised. And he was very happy that we got his favorite cake!

B PAIR WORK Compare your information with a partner.

This page is intentionally left blank

Grammar plus

UNIT 1

1 Past tense page 3

> ■ Use a form of be with born: I **was born** here. (NOT: I born here.) Don't use a form of be with the verb die: He **died** last year. (NOT: He was died last year.)

Complete the conversation.

1. **A:** Do you live around here?
   B: No, I don't. I'm from Costa Rica.
   A: Really? _Were you born_ in Costa Rica?
   B: No. Actually, I was born in San Miguelito, Panama.

2. **A:** That's interesting. So where _____?
   B: I grew up in Costa Rica. My family moved there when I was little.

3. **A:** _____ in the capital?
   B: No, my family didn't live in a city. We lived in a small town called Puerto Viejo.

4. **A:** _____ away from Puerto Viejo?
   B: Oh, about eight years ago. I left Puerto Viejo to go to college.

5. **A:** Where _____ to college?
   B: I went to college in San Jose, and I live there now.

6. **A:** And _____ to Miami?
   B: I got here a few days ago. I'm visiting my cousin.

2 Used to page 5

> ■ Use the base form of used to in questions and negative statements: Did you **use to** play sports? (NOT: Did you used to play sports?) I didn't **use to** like bananas. (NOT: I didn't used to like bananas.)
>
> ■ Don't use never in negative statements: I **never used to** wear sunglasses. (NOT: I never didn't use to wear sunglasses.)

Complete the conversations with the correct form of used to.

1. **A:** Hey, Dad. What kinds of clothes _did you use to_ wear – you know, when you were a kid?
   B: Oh, we _____ wear jeans and T-shirts – like you kids do now.
   A: Really? _____ Mom _____ dress like that, too?
   B: No, not really. She never _____ like wearing pants. She always _____ wear skirts and dresses.

2. **A:** _____ you _____ play a sport when you were a kid?
   B: Well, I _____ be a swimmer. My sister and I _____ swim on a team.
   A: Wow, that's cool! Were you good?
   B: Yeah. I _____ win gold medals all the time. And my sister _____ be the fastest swimmer on the team.

UNIT 2

1 Expressions of quantity `page 9`

■ Count nouns have a plural form that usually ends in -s. Noncount nouns don't have
a plural form because you can't separate and count them: Are there any **parking
garages** around here? BUT Is there any **parking** around here? (NOT: Are there any
~~parkings~~ around here?)

Complete the conversations with the correct words in parentheses.

1. A: There's _____ (too many / too much) traffic in this city. There should be
_____ (fewer / less) cars downtown.
B: The problem is there _____ (aren't / isn't) enough public transportation.
A: You're right. We should have more _____ (bus / buses). There
_____ (aren't / isn't) enough of them during rush hour.

2. A: How do you like your new neighborhood?
B: It's terrible, actually. There's _____ (too many / too much) noise and
_____ (too few / too little) parking.
A: That's too bad. There _____ (aren't / isn't) enough parking spaces in my
neighborhood either.

3. A: Did you hear about the changes to the city center? Starting next month, there will be more
bicycle _____ (lane / lanes) and _____ (fewer / less)
street parking.
B: That's good. There _____ (are too many / is too much) pollution downtown.
I'm sure there will be _____ (fewer / less) accidents, too.
A: That's true.

2 Indirect questions from Wh-questions `page 11`

■ Indirect questions are often polite requests for information. *Can you tell me
how much this magazine costs?* sounds more polite than *How much does this
magazine cost?*

Complete the conversation with indirect questions.

1. A: Excuse me. Can you _tell me where the post office is_ _____ ?
B: Yes, of course. The post office is on the next corner.

2. A: And could you _____ ?
B: You can find a really good restaurant on Central Avenue.

3. A: OK. Do you _____ ?
B: Yes. The restaurant is called Giorgio's.

4. A: Thanks. Can you _____ ?
B: Yes. They serve Italian food.

5. A: Oh, good! Do you _____ ?
B: It opens at 5:00. Tell them Joe sent you!
A: OK, Joe. Thanks for everything! Bye now.

Unit 2 Grammar plus **133**

1 Evaluations and comparisons page 17

> - In evaluations, *enough* goes after adjectives and before nouns.
> - adjective + *enough*: This house isn't **bright enough**. (NOT: This house isn't ~~enough bright~~.
> - noun + *enough*: This house doesn't have **enough light**. (NOT: This house doesn't have ~~light enough~~.)

A Read each situation. Then write two sentences describing the problem, one sentence with *not . . . enough* and one with *too*.

1. Our family needs a big house. This house is very small.
   a. This house isn't big enough for us.
   b. This house is too small for us.
2. We want to live on a quiet street. This street is very noisy.
   a. _____
   b. _____
3. We need three bedrooms. This house has only two.
   a. _____
   b. _____
4. We want a spacious living room. This one is cramped.
   a. _____
   b. _____

B Rewrite the comparisons using *as . . . as*. Use *just* when possible.

1. My new apartment is smaller than my old one.
    My new apartment isn't as large as my old one.
2. This neighborhood is safer than my old one.

   _____
3. This apartment has a lot of privacy. My old one did, too.

   _____
4. My rent is reasonable now. It was very high before.

   _____

2 *Wish* page 20

> - Use *could* (the past of *can*) and *would* (the past of *will*) with *wish*: I **can't** move right now, but I wish I **could**. My landlord **won't** paint my apartment, but I wish he **would**.

Match the problems with the wishes.

1. My house isn't very nice.   _c_   a. I wish I could find a good roommate.
2. It costs a lot to live here.   ____   b. I wish he'd return my calls.
3. My landlord won't call me back.   ____   c. I wish it were more attractive.
4. I have noisy neighbors.   ____   d. I wish I could afford a car.
5. I don't like living alone.   ____   e. I wish their music weren't so loud.
6. The buses don't run very often.   ____   f. I wish it weren't so expensive.

UNIT 4

1 Simple past vs. present perfect page 23

■ Use the simple past – not the present perfect – when you say when an event ended:
I had sushi last night. (NOT: I've had sushi last night.)

Complete the conversations. Choose the best forms.

1. A: What _____ (did you have / have you had) for dinner last
night?

   B: I _____ (tried / have tried) Indian food for the first time.
_____ (Did you ever have / Have you ever had) it?

   A: A friend and I _____ (ate / have eaten) at an Indian
restaurant just last week. It _____ (was / has been)
delicious!

2. A: _____ (Did you ever take / Have you ever taken)
a cooking class?

   B: No, I _____ (didn't / haven't). How about you?

   A: I _____ (took / have taken) a few classes. My last
class _____ (was / has been) in December. We
_____ (learned / have learned) how to make some
wonderful Spanish dishes.

3. A: I _____ (watched / have watched) a great cooking show
on TV yesterday.

   B: Really? I _____ (never saw / have never seen) a cooking
show. _____ (Was it / Has it been) boring?

   A: No, it _____ (wasn't / hasn't). It _____
(was / has been) very interesting!

2 Sequence adverbs page 25

■ *Then, next,* and *after that* mean the same. *First* comes first, and *finally* comes last; you
can use the other adverbs in any order: **First,** put some water in a pan. **Then/Next/
After that,** put the eggs in the water. **Finally,** boil the eggs for 7 minutes.

Unscramble the steps in this recipe for hamburgers. Then write the steps in order.

salt and pepper   add   in the bowl   to the meat   then

_____ : _____

2 pounds of chopped beef   put in a bowl   first,

 Step 1   : _First, put 2 pounds of chopped beef in a bowl._____

put   the burgers   in a pan   finally,   and cook for 10 minutes

_____ : _____

next,   the meat   and the salt and pepper   mix   together

_____ : _____

into four burgers   after that,   with your hands   form the meat

_____ : _____

Unit 4 Grammar plus **135**

1 Future with *be going to* and *will* 　page 31

> ■ Use the base form of the verb – not the infinitive (*to* + base form) – with *will*:
> I think I**'ll go** to Hawaii next winter. (NOT: I think I'll ~~to~~ go to Hawaii next winter.)
>
> ■ Use *be going to* – not *will* – when you know something is going to happen:
> Look at those black clouds. It**'s going to** rain. (NOT: It ~~will~~ rain.)

Complete the conversation with the correct form of *be going to* or *will* and the verbs in parentheses.

A: It's Friday – at last! What _are you going to do_____ (do) this weekend?

B: I'm not sure. I'm really tired, so I probably _____ (not do) anything exciting. Maybe I _____ (see) a movie on Saturday. How about you? How _____ (spend) your weekend?

A: My wife and I _____ (do) some work on our house. We _____ (paint) the living room on Saturday. On Sunday, we _____ (clean) all the rugs.

B: _____ (do) anything fun?

A: Oh, I think we _____ (have) a lot of fun. We like working around the house. And Sunday's my birthday, so we _____ (have) dinner at my favorite Italian restaurant.

B: Now that sounds like fun!

2 Modals for necessity and suggestion 　page 33

> ■ Some modals for necessity and suggestion are stronger than others.
> Weak (for advice or an opinion): *should, ought to*
> Stronger (for a warning): *had better*
> Strongest (for an obligation): *must, need to, have to*

Choose the correct word or words to complete the advice to travelers.

1. You _____ (must / should) show identification at the airport. They won't allow you on a plane without an official ID.

2. Your ID _____ (needs to / ought to) have a picture of you on it. It's required.

3. The picture of you _____ (has to / ought to) be recent. They won't accept an old photo.

4. Travelers _____ (must / should) get to the airport at least two hours before their flight. It's not a good idea to get there later than that.

5. All travelers _____ (have to / had better) go through airport security. It's necessary for passenger safety.

6. Many airlines don't serve food, so passengers on long flights probably _____ (must / ought to) buy something to eat at the airport.

1 Two-part verbs; *will* for responding to requests page 37

- Two-part verbs are verb + particle.
- If the object of a two-part verb is a noun, the noun can come before or after the particle: **Take out** the trash./**Take** the trash **out**.
- If the object is a pronoun, the pronoun must come before the particle: **Take** it **out**. (NOT: Take ~~out it~~.)

Write conversations. First, rewrite the request given by changing the position of the particle. Then write a response to the request using *it* or *them*.

1. Put away your clothes, please.
   A: <u>Put your clothes away, please.</u>
   B: <u>OK. I'll put them away.</u>
2. Turn the lights on, please.
   A: _____
   B: _____
3. Please turn your music down.
   A: _____
   B: _____
4. Clean up the kitchen, please.
   A: _____
   B: _____
5. Turn off your phone, please.
   A: _____
   B: _____

2 Requests with modals and *Would you mind . . . ?* page 39

- Use the base form of the verb – not the infinitive (*to* + base form) – with the modals *can*, *could*, and *would*: **Could** you **get** me a sandwich? (NOT: Could you ~~to~~ get me a sandwich?)
- Requests with modals and *Would you mind . . . ?* are polite – even without *please*. *Can you get me a sandwich?* sounds much more polite than *Get me a sandwich*.

Change these sentences to polite requests. Use the words in parentheses.

1. Bring in the mail. (could)
   <u>Could you bring in the mail?</u>
2. Put your shoes by the door. (would you mind)
   _____
3. Don't leave dishes in the sink. (would you mind)
   _____
4. Change the TV channel. (can)
   _____

5. Don't play ball inside. (would you mind)
   _____
6. Clean up your mess. (would you mind)
   _____
7. Put away the clean towels. (can)
   _____
8. Pick up your things. (could)
   _____

UNIT 7

1 Infinitives and gerunds for uses and purposes ◢ page 45

- Sentences with infinitives and gerunds mean the same: *I use my cell phone to send text messages* means the same as *I use my cell phone for sending text messages*.
- Use a gerund – not an infinitive – after *for*: Satellites are used **for studying** weather. (NOT: Satellites are used for ~~to study~~ weather.)

Read each sentence about a technology item. Write two sentences about the item's use and purpose. Use the information in parentheses.

1. My sister's car has a built-in GPS system. (She use / get directions)
   a. *She uses the GPS system to get directions.*
   b. *She uses the GPS system for getting directions.*
2. I love my new smartphone. (I use / take pictures)
   a. _____
   b. _____
3. That's a flash drive. (You use / back up files)
   a. _____
   b. _____
4. My little brother wants his own laptop. (He would only use / watch movies and play games)
   a. _____
   b. _____
5. I'm often on my computer all day long. (I use / shop online and do research)
   a. _____
   b. _____

2 Imperatives and infinitives for giving suggestions ◢ page 47

- With imperatives and infinitives, *not* goes before – not after – to: Try **not to** talk too long. (NOT: Try ~~to not~~ talk too long.)

Rewrite the sentences as suggestions. Use the words in parentheses.

1. When you go to the movies, turn off your phone. (don't forget)
   When you go to the movies, don't forget to turn off your phone.
2. Don't talk on the phone when you're in an elevator. (try)
   _____
3. Don't eat or drink anything when you're at the computer. (be sure)
   _____
4. Clean your computer screen and keyboard once a week. (remember)
   _____
5. Don't use your tablet outside when it's raining. (make sure)
   _____
6. When the bell rings to start class, put your music player away! (be sure)
   _____

UNIT 8

1 Relative clauses of time page 51

> ■ Relative clauses with *when* describe the word *time* or a noun that refers to a period of time, such as *day, night, month,* and *year.*

Combine the two sentences using *when.*

1. Thanksgiving is a holiday. Entire families get together.
  Thanksgiving is a holiday when entire families get together.

2. It's a wonderful time. People give thanks for the good things in their lives.
  _____

3. It's a day. Everyone eats much more than usual.
  _____

4. I remember one particular year. The whole family came to our house.
  _____

5. That year was very cold. It snowed all Thanksgiving day.
  _____

6. I remember another thing about that Thanksgiving. My brother and I baked eight pies.
  _____

2 Adverbial clauses of time page 54

> ■ An adverbial clause of time can come before or after the main clause. When it comes before the main clause, use a comma. When it comes after the main clause, don't use a comma: When Ginny and Tom met, they both lived in San Juan. BUT: Ginny and Tom met when they both lived in San Juan.
> ■ The words *couple* and *family* are collective nouns. They are usually used with singular verbs: When a couple **gets** married, they often receive gifts. (NOT: When a couple ~~get~~ married, they often receive gifts.)

Combine the two sentences using the adverb in parentheses. Write one sentence with the adverbial clause before the main clause and another with the adverbial clause after the main clause.

1. Students complete their courses. A school holds a graduation ceremony. (after)
  a. *After students complete their courses, a school holds a graduation ceremony.*
  b. *A school holds a graduation ceremony after students complete their courses.*

2. Students gather to put on robes and special hats. The ceremony starts. (before)
  a. _____
  b. _____

3. Music plays. The students walk in a line to their seats. (when)
  a. _____
  b. _____

4. School officials and teachers make speeches. Students get their diplomas. (after)
  a. _____
  b. _____

5. The ceremony is finished. Students throw their hats into the air and cheer. (when)
  a. _____
  b. _____

Grammar plus answer key

Unit 1

1 Past tense
2. did you grow up/are you from
3. Did you live
4. When did you move
5. did you go
6. when did you come/get

2 Used to
1. A: Hey, Dad. What kinds of clothes **did you use to** wear – you know, when you were a kid?
   B: Oh, we **used to** wear jeans and T-shirts – like you kids do now.
   A: Really? **Did** Mom **use to** dress like that, too?
   B: No, not really. She never **used to** like wearing pants. She always **used to** wear skirts and dresses.
2. A: **Did** you **use to** play a sport when you were a kid?
   B: Well, I **used to** be a swimmer. My sister and I **used to** swim on a team.
   A: Wow, that's cool! Were you good?
   B: Yeah. I **used to** win gold medals all the time. And my sister **used to** be the fastest swimmer on the team.

Unit 2

1 Expressions of quantity
1. A: There's **too much** traffic in this city. There should be **fewer** cars downtown.
   B: The problem is there **isn't** enough public transportation.
   A: You're right. We should have more **buses**. There **aren't** enough of them during rush hour.
2. A: How do you like your new neighborhood?
   B: It's terrible, actually. There's **too much** noise and **too little** parking.
   A: That's too bad. There **aren't** enough parking spaces in my neighborhood either.
3. A: Did you hear about the changes to the city center? Starting next month, there will be more bicycle **lanes** and **less** street parking.
   B: That's good. There **is too much** pollution downtown. I'm sure there will be **fewer** accidents, too.
   A: That's true.

2 Indirect questions from *Wh*-questions
Answers may vary. Some possible answers:
2. And could you **tell me where I can find a good restaurant**?
3. Do you **know what the name of the restaurant is**?
4. Can you **tell me what type of food they serve**?
5. Do you **know what time the restaurant opens**?

Unit 3

1 Evaluations and comparisons
A
Answers may vary. Some possible answers:
2. This street isn't quiet enough./This street is too noisy.
3. This house doesn't have enough bedrooms./This house is too small for us./This house has too few bedrooms for us.
4. This living room isn't spacious enough./This living room doesn't have enough space./This living room is too cramped/small.
B
Answers may vary. Some possible answers:
2. My old neighborhood isn't as safe as this one.
3. This apartment has (just) as much privacy as my old one.
4. My rent isn't as high as it used to be.

2 Wish
2. f   3. b   4. e   5. a   6. d

Unit 4

1 Simple past vs. present perfect
1. A: What **did you have** for dinner last night?
   B: I **tried** Indian food for the first time. **Have you ever had** it?
   A: A friend and I **ate** at an Indian restaurant just last week. It **was** delicious!
2. A: **Have you ever taken** a cooking class?
   B: No, **I haven't**. How about you?
   A: I **have taken** a few classes. My last class **was** in December. We **learned** how to make some wonderful Spanish dishes.
3. A: I **watched** a great cooking show on TV yesterday.
   B: Really? I **have never seen** a cooking show. **Was it** boring?
   A: No, it **wasn't**. It **was** very interesting!

2 Sequence adverbs
Step 1: First, put 2 pounds of chopped beef in a bowl.
Step 2: Then add salt and pepper to the meat in the bowl.
Step 3: Next, mix the meat and the salt and pepper together.
Step 4: After that, form the meat into four burgers with your hands.
Step 5: Finally, put the burgers in a pan and cook for 10 minutes.

Unit 5

1 Future with *be going to* and *will*

B: I'm not sure. I'm really tired, so I probably **won't do** anything exciting. Maybe I**'ll see** a movie on Saturday. How about you? How **are you going to spend** your weekend?

A: My wife and I **are going to do** some work on our house. We**'re going to paint** the living room on Saturday. On Sunday, we**'re going to clean** all the rugs.

B: **Are(n't) you going to do** anything fun?

A: Oh, I think we**'ll have/'re going to have** a lot of fun. We like working around the house. And Sunday's my birthday, so we**'re going to have** dinner at my favorite Italian restaurant.

B: Now that sounds like fun!

2 Modals for necessity and suggestions

1. You **must** show identification at the airport. They won't allow you on a plane without an official ID.
2. Your ID **needs to** have a picture of you on it. It's required.
3. The picture of you **has to** be recent. They won't accept an old photo.
4. Travelers **should** get to the airport at least two hours before their flight. It's not a good idea to get there later than that.
5. All travelers **have to** go through airport security. It's necessary for passenger safety.
6. Many airlines don't serve food, so passengers on long flights probably **ought to** buy something to eat at the airport.

Unit 6

1 Two-part verbs; *will* for responding to requests

2. A: Turn on the lights, please.
   B: OK. I'll turn them on.
3. A: Please turn down your music.
   B: OK. I'll turn it down.
4. A: Clean the kitchen up, please.
   B: OK. I'll clean it up.
5. A: Turn your phone off, please.
   B: OK. I'll turn it off.

2 Requests with modals and *Would you mind . . . ?*

2. Would you mind putting your shoes by the door?
3. Would you mind not leaving dishes in the sink?
4. Can you change the TV channel?
5. Would you mind not playing ball inside?
6. Would you mind cleaning up your mess?
7. Can you put away the clean towels?
8. Could you pick up your things?

Unit 7

1 Infinitives and gerunds for uses and purposes

2. a. I use my smartphone/it to take pictures.
   b. I use my smartphone/it for taking pictures.
3. a. You use a flash drive/it to back up files.
   b. You use a flash drive/it for backing up files.
4. a. He would only use a laptop/it to watch movies and play games.
   b. He would only use a laptop/it for watching movies and playing games.
5. a. I use my computer/it to shop online and do research.
   b. I use my computer/it for shopping online and doing research.

2 Imperatives and infinitives for giving suggestions

2. Try not to talk on the phone when you're in an elevator.
3. Be sure not to eat or drink anything when you're at the computer.
4. Remember to clean your computer screen and keyboard once a week.
5. Make sure not to use your tablet outside when it's raining.
6. When the bell rings to start class, be sure to put your music player away!

Unit 8

1 Relative clauses of time

2. It's a wonderful time when people give thanks for the good things in their lives.
3. It's a day when everyone eats much more than usual.
4. I remember one particular year when the whole family came to our house.
5. That year was very cold when it snowed all Thanksgiving day.
6. I remember another thing about that Thanksgiving when my brother and I baked eight pies.

2 Adverbial clauses of time

2. a. Before the ceremony starts, students gather to put on robes and special hats.
   b. Students gather to put on robes and special hats before the ceremony starts.
3. a. When music plays, the students walk in a line to their seats.
   b. The students walk in a line to their seats when music plays.
4. a. After school officials and teachers make speeches, students get their diplomas.
   b. Students get their diplomas after school officials and teachers make speeches.
5. a. When the ceremony is finished, students throw their hats into the air and cheer.
   b. Students throw their hats into the air and cheer when the ceremony is finished.

Credits

The authors and publishers acknowledge the following sources of copyright material and are grateful for the permissions granted. While every effort has been made, it has not always been possible to identify the sources of all the material used, or to trace all copyright holders. If any omissions are brought to our notice, we will be happy to include the appropriate acknowledgements on reprinting and in the next update to the digital edition, as applicable.

Texts

Text on p. 13 adapted from "The 4 Happiest Cities on Earth" by Ford Cochran. Copyright © National Geographic Creative. Reproduced with permission; Mark Boyle for the text on p. 21 adapted from "Living without money changed my way of being." Reproduced with kind permission of Mark Boyle; Text on p. 41 adapted from "World's weirdest hotel requests and complaints" by James Teideman. Copyright © www.skyscanner.net. Reproduced with kind permission.

Key: B = Below, BC = Below Centre, BL = Below Left, BR = Below Right, B/G = Background, C = Centre, CL = Centre Left, CR = Centre Right, L = Left, R = Right, T = Top, TC = Top Centre, TL = Top Left, TR = Top Right.

Illustrations

337 Jon (KJA Artists): 39, 92(B), 97; **Mark Duffin**: 18, 25(C), 37, 43(T); **Pablo Gallego** (Beehive Illustration): 43(B); **Thomas Girard** (Good Illustration): 2, 22, 41, 93; **John Goodwin** (Eye Candy Illustration): 40; **Daniel Gray**: 75, 118, 120; **Quino Marin** (The Organisation): 36, 80, 128; **Gavin Reece** (New Division): 58, 81, 119; **Paul Williams** (Sylvie Poggio Artists): 16, 114.

Photos

Back cover (woman with whiteboard): Jenny Acheson/Stockbyte/GettyImages; Back cover (whiteboard): Nemida/GettyImages; Back cover (man using phone): Betsie Van Der Meer/Taxi/GettyImages; Back cover (woman smiling): PeopleImages.com/DigitalVision/GettyImages; Back cover (name tag): Tetra Images/GettyImages; Back cover (handshake): David Lees/Taxi/GettyImages; p. v (TL): Hero Images/Getty Images; p. v (TR): Cultura RM Exclusive/dotdotred/Getty Images; p. v (CL): vitchanan/iStock/Getty Images Plus/Getty Images; p. v (CR): Svetlana Braun/iStock/Getty Images Plus/Getty Images; p. v (BL): Hero Images/Getty Images; p. v (BR): Cultura RM Exclusive/dotdotred/Getty Images; p. vi (Unit 1), p. 2 (header): Ekaterina Borner/Moment Open/Getty Images; p. 2 (TL): Juanmonino/E+/Getty Images; p. 2 (TR): Purestock/Getty Images; p. 6 (TR): GlobalStock/E+/Getty Images; p. 5 (T): JGI/Jamie Grill/Blend Images/Getty Images; p. 5 (T): Maskot/Maskot/Getty Images; p. 6 (CL): Alistair Berg/DigitalVision/Getty Images; p. 7 (TL): Bettmann/Getty Images; p. 7 (BR): Alberto Pizzoli/AFP/Getty Images; p. vi (Unit 2), p. 8 (header): Martin Polsson/Maskot/Getty Images; p. 8 (traffic jam): Roevin/Moment/Getty Images; p. 8 (green space): Yutthana Jantong/EyeEm/Getty Images; p. 8 (Ex 2a.b): Sergiy Serdyuk/Hemera/Getty Images Plus/Getty Images; p. 8 (Ex 2a.b): AvalancheZ/iStock/Getty Images Plus/Getty Images; p. 8 (Ex 2a.c): Peeterv/iStock/Getty Images Plus/Getty Images; p. 8 (microphone): Darryn van der Walt/Moment/Getty Images; p. 9: Kentaroo Tryman/Maskot/Getty Images; p. 10: arnaudbertrande/RooM/Getty Images; p. 11: Tim Bieber/Photodisc/Getty Images; p. 13 (photo 1): peder77/iStock/Getty Images Plus/Getty Images; p. 13 (photo 2): Sollina Images/The Image Bank/Getty Images; p. 13 (photo 3): Caiaimage/Paul Bradbury/Getty Images; p. 13 (photo 4): Jonathan Drake/Bloomberg/Getty Images; p. 14: Three Lions/Stringer/Getty Images; p. 15: Mark Edward Atkinson/Blend Images/Getty Images; p. vi (Unit 3), p. 16 (header): Hill Street Studios/Blend Images/Getty Images; p. 16 (BR): Lihee Avidan/Photonica World/Getty Images; p. 17 (L): Leren Lu/Taxi/Getty Images; p. 17 (R): Aliyev Alexei Sergeevich/Blend Images/Getty Images; p. 18: Coneyl Jay/Stockbyte/Getty Images; p. 19 (T): Iaflor/iStock/Getty Images Plus/Getty Images; p. 19 (B): Westend61/Getty Images; p. 20: Jose Luis Pelaez Inc/Blend Images/Getty Images; p. 21: © Mark Boyle; p. vi (Unit 4), p. 22 (header): Yuri_Arcurs/DigitalVision/Getty Images; p. 22 (L): Anna Pustynnikova/iStock/Getty Images Plus/Getty Images; p. 22 (CL): John Ibarra Photography/Moment/Getty Images; p. 22 (CR): PuspaSwara/iStock/Getty Images Plus/Getty Images; p. 22 (R): trindade51/iStock/Getty Images Plus/Getty Images; p. 22 (B): David Stuart/Getty Images; p. 23: Dan Dalton/DigitalVision/Getty Images; p. 24 (TR): bdspn/iStock/Getty Images Plus/Getty Images; p. 24 (bake): Mark_KA/iStock/Getty Images Plus/Getty Images; p. 24 (boil): Dorling Kindersley/Getty Images; p. 24 (fry): Chris Everard/The Image Bank/Getty Images; p. 24 (grill): Dave Bradley Photography/The Image Bank/Getty Images; p. 24 (roast): Lew Robertson/Photographer's Choice/Getty Images; p. 24 (steam): Aberration Films Ltd/Science Photo Library/Getty Images; p. 25 (TR): Lauri Patterson/E+/Getty Images; p. 25 (photo 1): Simon Wheeler Ltd/Photolibrary/Getty Images; p. 25 (photo 2): jacktherabbit/iStock/Getty Images Plus/Getty Images; p. 25 (photo 3): Dave King/Dorling Kindersley/Getty Images; p. 25 (photo 4): Bruce James/StockFood Creative/Getty Images; p. 25 (photo 5): robdoss/iStock/Getty Images Plus/Getty Images; p. 26 (spaghetti): Lauri Patterson/E+/Getty Images; p. 26 (cookies): 4kodiak/E+/Getty Images; p. 26 (salsa): Douglas Johns/StockFood Creative/Getty Images; p. 26 (toast): DebbiSmirnoff/iStock/Getty Images Plus/Getty Images; p. 26 (popcorn): Michael Deuson/Photolibrary/Getty Images; p. 26 (CR): Plattform/Getty Images; p. 26 (BL): AD077/iStock/Getty Images Plus/Getty Images; p. 27 (TR): stevecoleimages/E+/Getty Images; p. 27 (BL): Lombardis Pizza of New York City; p. 29 (CR): Lauri Patterson/E+/Getty Images; p. 29 (BR): Echo/Cultura/Getty Images; p. vi (Unit 5), p. 30 (header): Hero Images/Getty Images; p. 30 (Ex 1: photo 1): Gary John Norman/Cultura Exclusive/Getty Images; p. 30 (Ex 1: photo 2): Yuri_Arcurs/DigitalVision/Getty Images; p. 30 (Ex 1: photo 3): LuckyBusiness/iStock/Getty Images Plus/Getty Images; p. 30 (Ex 1: photo 4): Yellow Dog Productions/The Image Bank/Getty Images; p. 30 (BR): AID/a.collectionRF/Getty Images; p. 31: Ed Freeman/The Image Bank/Getty Images; p. 33: AngiePhotos/E+/Getty Images; p. 34 (CR): John W Banagan/Photographer's Choice/Getty Images; p. 34 (BR): annebaek/iStock/Getty Images Plus/Getty Images; p. 35 (photo 1): Brian Bailey/The Image Bank/Getty Images; p. 35 (photo 2): Matteo Colombo/Moment/Getty Images; p. 35 (photo 3): Adam Woolfitt/robertharding/Getty Images; p. vi (Unit 6), p. 36 (header): B and G Images/Photographer's Choice/Getty Images; p. 36 (TL): Westend61/Getty Images; p. 38 (CR): Stockbyte/Getty Images; p. 38 (BR): DragonImages/iStock/Getty Images Plus/Getty Images; p. 42: Rudi Von Briel/Photolibrary/Getty Images; p. 44 (header): anyaivanova/iStock/Getty Images Plus/Getty Images; p. 44 (TR): MixAll Studio/Blend Images/Getty Images; p. 45: monkeybusinessimages/iStock/Getty Images Plus/Getty Images; p. 46 (CR): scyther5/iStock/Getty Images Plus/Getty Images; p. 46 (BR): Michele Falzone/AWL Images/Getty Images; p. 47: Maskot/Getty Images; p. 48 (speaker): Atsadej0819/iStock/Getty Images Plus/Getty Images; p. 48 (GPS): Peter Dazeley/Photographer's Choice/Getty Images; p. 48 (flash drive): Westend61/Getty Images; p. 48 (smartphone): milindri/iStock/Getty Images Plus/Getty Images; p. 48 (ATM): Volodymyr Krasyuk/iStock/Getty Images Plus/Getty Images; p. 49: Daren Woodward/iStock/Getty Images Plus/Getty Images; p. vi (Unit 8), p. 50 (header): ferrantraite/E+/Getty Images; p. 50 (Saint Patrick's Day): Sachin Polassery/Moment Editorial/Getty Images; p. 50 (Day of the Dead): Darryl Leniuk/Photographer's Choice/Getty Images; p. 50 (Chinese New year): WILLIAM WEST/AFP/Getty Images; p. 50 (Thanksgiving): Kathryn Russell Studios/Photolibrary/Getty Images; p. 51 (L): Hero Images/Getty Images; p. 51 (C): JGI/Jamie Grill/Blend Images/Getty Images; p. 51 (R): Blend Images – JGI/Jamie Grill/Brand X Pictures/Getty Images; p. 52 (TL): altrendo images/Getty Images; p. 52 (CR): Thinkstock Images/Stockbyte/Getty Images; p. 52 (B): huzu1959/Moment Open/Getty Images; p. 53 (Julia): Tara Moore/Stone/Getty Images; p. 53 (Anusha): Carlina Teteris/Moment/Getty Images; p. 53 (TR): Blend Images/Getty Images; p. 54: Tetra Images/Getty Images; p. 55 (TL): oversnap/iStock/Getty Images Plus/Getty Images; p. 55 (BR): ruslan117/iStock/Getty Images Plus/Getty Images; p. 56 (CR): vgajic/iStock/Getty Images Plus/Getty Images; p. 57 (TL): Dezein/iStock/Getty Images Plus/Getty Images; p. 57 (TC): artpartner-images/Photographer's Choice/Getty Images; p. 57 (TR): André Rieck/EyeEmGetty Images; p. 57 (BR): Satoshi Kawase/Moment/Getty Images; p. 115 (TL): DC_Colombia/iStock/Getty Images Plus/Getty Images; p. 115 (TR): Rob Carr/Getty Images; p. 115 (BL): Sylvester Adams/DigitalVision/Getty Images; p. 115 (BR): 9Tiw/iStock/Getty Images Plus/Getty Images; p. 116: Paul Burns/DigitalVision/Getty Images; p. 117: Jon Feingersh/Blend Images/Getty Images; p. 118: Vince Cavataio/Design Pics/Perspectives/Getty Images; p. 120: Michele Falzone/Photographer's Choice/Getty Images; p. 121 (TL): Yellow Dog Productions/The Image Bank/Getty Images; p. 121 (TR): Klaus Vedfelt/DigitalVision/Getty Images; p. 121 (CL): Susan Chiang/E+/Getty Images; p. 121 (CR): Nick White and Fiona Jackson-Downes/Cultura/Getty Images; p. 121 (BL): Steve Debenport/iStock/Getty Images Plus/Getty Images; p. 121 (BR): Celia Peterson/arabianEye/Getty Images; p. 122 (BL): Jon Feingersh/Blend Images/Getty Images; p. 122 (BC): Blend Images-Jose Luis Pelaez Inc/Brand X Pictures/Getty Images; p. 122 (BR): Westend61/Getty Images.